NEW DIRECTIONS
FOR METHODOLOGY OF
BEHAVIORAL SCIENCE

Number 2 • 1979

NEW DIRECTIONS FOR METHODOLOGY OF BEHAVIORAL SCIENCE

A Quarterly Sourcebook
Donald W. Fiske, Editor-in-Chief

Number 2, 1979

Methods for Studying Person–Situation Interactions

Lynn R. Kahle
Guest Editor

Jossey-Bass Inc., Publishers
San Francisco • Washington • London

METHODS FOR STUDYING PERSON–SITUATION INTERACTIONS
New Directions for Methodology of Behavioral Science
Number 2, 1979
     Lynn R. Kahle, Guest Editor

New Directions for Methodology of Behavioral Science is published
quarterly by Jossey-Bass Inc., Publishers. Subscriptions are available
at the regular rate for institutions, libraries, and agencies
of $25 for one year. Individuals may subscribe at the special
professional rate of $15 for one year.

Correspondence:
Subscriptions, single-issue orders, change of address notices,
undelivered copies, and other correspondence should be sent to
New Directions Subscriptions, Jossey-Bass Inc., Publishers,
433 California Street, San Francisco, California 94104.
Editorial correspondence should be sent to the Editor-in-Chief,
Donald W. Fiske, University of Chicago, Chicago, Illinois 60637.

Library of Congress Catalogue Card Number LC 78-73930

Cover design by Willi Baum
Manufactured in the United States of America

Contents

Editor's Notes   Lynn R. Kahle   **vii**

Assessing Persons and Situations with the   Daryl J. Bem   **1**
Template Matching Technique

The template matching technique allows researchers to measure persons and situations, the independent variables of interactionism, commensurately.

Cross-Lagged Panel Correlation   Lynn R. Kahle   **17**
and Personality   John J. Berman

A whole new vista opens up when you select a different statistical treatment for independent variables.

Assessing Interpersonal Relationships   Donald R. Peterson   **33**
in Natural Settings

If *interaction* means a process rather than an event, the way to measure it changes from looking at individuals to looking at individuals in interpersonal relations.

Interaction as Person-Environment Fit   Richard A. Kulka   **55**

One statistical concept of interaction implies that the types of interaction vary far more widely than many people assume.

Personality and Behavioral Prediction: James Jaccard   **73**
An Analysis of Behavioral
Criterion Measures

Behavior, the dependent variable in most interactionism research, involves far more assumptions and forms than researchers often recognize.

Epistemology, Metaphysics, and   Harold L. Raush   **93**
Person-Situation Methodology:
Conclusions

Numerous continua help discriminate among the philosophic implications of the methods proposed in this sourcebook and other alternative approaches.

Index   **107**

Editor's Notes

The concept of person-situation interactions is not new as a theoretical construct, but its recent re-emerging popularity has resulted more from a response to data than from vague speculation about what ought to be. Specifically, personality researchers have grown acutely aware of the failure of their measures to account for large amounts of variance and of the need to expand their scope of inquiry. At the same time researchers who have devoted all of their attention to situations have also recognized the need to expand the scope of their inquiry to allow them to account for sizable contributions to variance on significant topics. Both personologists and situationists have discovered that the other has something of value; the dialectic between the personologist and the situationist has nudged each toward a synthesis called person-situation interactionism. The new interactionist seeks to account for important amounts of variance on important topics through simultaneously considering persons and situations. Thus the personologist welcomes the situationist to the "real world," and the situationist welcomes the personologist to "real science."

Although the concept of person-situation interactions has recently been quite useful for integrating the best ideas and data from these antagonists, a number of critics have convincingly argued that most popular methodologies such as ANOVA designs and traditional correlation techniques have failed to illuminate the processes involved in person-situation interactions. The answer to the fundamental question of *how* person-situation interactions influence behavior must await methodological innovation—method must catch up with theory. The purpose of this sourcebook is to gather in one place information about some of the more promising innovative methods for studying person-situation interactions, in order to stimulate a methodological dialectic.

The first chapters in this sourcebook deal with the independent variables in person-situation interactions, persons and situations. Bem attacks one problem that perplexed previous researchers: how to measure persons and situations on commensurate dimensions. Bem describes the template-matching technique for resolving this conflict with Q-sort data. Kahle and Berman take a different problem and describe a statistical procedure for dealing with independent variables that cannot be manipulated easily. But if one applies the technique they propose, some variables that are viewed as independent when a research project begins may very well end up as dependent variables afterwards!

The second pair of chapters examine what goes on between the introduction of the independent variables and the measurement of the dependent variables, namely interaction. Peterson argues that interaction is a process rather than static, and describes how he measures the interaction process. Kulka takes a more statistical approach to the concept of interaction, conceiving of interaction as a measure of fit between person and environment. This line of thinking identifies some problems with simplistic interaction concepts.

Jaccard's chapter probes the concept of behavior as it is used in person-situation interaction research; he points to the importance of examining what one means by *behavior* when deciding to use it as a dependent variable. Thus, one section of this sourcebook deals with each of the three phases of a typical study—independent variable measurement, the intervening interaction, and dependent variable measurement.

In the concluding chapter Raush identifies several bipolar continua that help to place the wide range of the preceding chapters into a philosophic context. In addition he describes his ideal interactive paradigm. It becomes clear that the concept of person-situation interactions touches a remarkably diverse set of methodological, theoretical, and substantive areas of psychology. Raush and Kulka (and to some degree, the other authors as well) selected references especially to represent the most important sources of information on person-situation methodology. The neophyte interactionist would do well to consult Endler and Magnusson's (1976) book for a history of the controversy and Magnusson and Endler's (1977) for recent statements by principal methodologists. The *American Psychologist* published a good example of the methodology dialectic recently (Hogan, DeSoto, and Solano, 1977; Mischel, 1977). Finally, two of the editor's favorite recent contributions somehow escaped mention elsewhere (Duncan and Fiske, 1977; McGuire and Padawer-Singer, 1976).

Several themes emerge. First, it is quite realistic to assume that the ".30 correlation barrier" can be broken: we *can* obtain correlations greater than .30 in person-situation interaction research. Any one of the techniques alone could probably generate higher correlations, and in fact most have. By combining several of these techniques in one study, the correlations may well be impressive indeed.

A second theme is the close intertwining of method and theory. Perhaps Peterson's chapter best illustrates how one concept of person-situation interactions simply could not be studied with traditional techniques. As new ideas develop from discussions of person-situation interactions, new methods will have to be developed to study those topics. Meanwhile, those here described certainly warrant attention.

Lynn R. Kahle
Guest Editor

References

Duncan, Jr., S., and Fiske, D. W. *Face-to-face Interaction: Research, Methods and Theory.* Hillsdale, N.J.: Erlbaum, 1977.

Endler, N. S., and Magnusson, D. (Eds.). *Interactional Psychology and Personality.* New York: Wiley, 1976.

Hogan, R., DeSoto, C. B., and Solano, C. "Traits, Tests, and Personality Research." *American Psychologist,* 1977, *32,* 255–264.

McGuire, W. J., and Padawer-Singer, A. "Trait Salience in the Spontaneous Self-Concept." *Journal of Personality and Social Psychology.* 1976, *33,* 743–754.

Magnusson, D., and Endler, N. S. (Eds.). *Personality at the Crossroads: Current Issues in Interactional Psychology.* Hillsdale, N.J.: Erlbaum, 1977.

Mischel, W. "On the Future of Personality Measurement." *American Psychologist,* 1977, *32,* 246–254.

Lynn R. Kahle is a postdoctoral fellow at the Institute for Social Research, University of Michigan.

The template matching technique, a new assessment method, provides a way of characterizing persons and situations in commensurate terms and enables investigators to probe the ecological validity of experimental settings as well as to test competing theories of particular situations against one another.

Assessing Persons and Situations with the Template Matching Technique

Daryl J. Bem

As the existence of this sourcebook affirms, the old maxim that behavior is a function of both the person and the situation is finally receiving more than lip service from psychologists. After years of assessing persons, many investigators are now beginning to assess situations as well (Frederiksen, 1972; Moos, 1973; and Pervin, 1978), and person-situation interaction is now a central topic in personality psychology (Endler and Magnusson, 1976; Magnusson and Endler, 1977).

None of the current assessment methods, however, uses a language of description that could be employed satisfactorily to characterize both persons and situations in a directly commensurate way. The development of such a common descriptive system is an important step toward a coherent theory of person-situation interaction, and this has been the goal of our own recent research efforts. The approach we have developed, the template matching technique, is actually just a formalization of a procedure that people use in everyday life when asked to describe a situation (Bem and Funder, 1978).

Consider, for example, a student who wants to know how he or she would fare at a particular college. This is a genuine problem in person-situation interaction in that the student is not interested in his or her potential performance at colleges in general, or in how students in general do at this particular college; what the student seeks is information about how his or her unique characteristics mesh or interact with the unique characteristics of that particular college. Accordingly, one particularly useful way to give this student information about the college is to describe how several types of students fare there: "Students with varied interests tend to get caught up in extracurricular activities, have a marvelous college experience, but get rather poor grades; students who work hard, but who are somewhat shy obtain good grades but are unlikely to have much interaction with the faculty; students who . . . ", and so forth. With this kind of description in hand, the student has only to match his or her own characteristics to the various "templates" we have provided in order to predict his or her probable outcomes at the college. Rather than describing the college in terms of the physical plant, faculty-student ratios, graduation requirements, and so forth, we have instead characterized it in terms of a set of template-outcome, or template-behavior pairs. The language system used to characterize the situation is the same system the student uses to characterize him or herself.

What we have proposed formally, then, is that situations be characterized as sets of template-behavior pairs, each template being a personality description of an idealized "type" of person expected to behave in a specified way in that setting. One then predicts the behavior of particular persons, in that setting, by comparing their own personality descriptions to each template in turn; and predicting that they will display the behavior associated with the template of closest match or greatest similarity.

Constructing the Templates

In order to operationalize the template construct, we have employed the Q-sort technique, utilizing the items of the California Q-Set devised by Jack Block (1978). Because this item set was originally designed for use by professionally trained clinicians, we have modified it for layperson use. (All Q-sort materials used in our research and the book by Block (1978) are available from Consulting Psychologists Press, 577 College Avenue, Palo Alto, California 94306.) The Q-set consists of 100 descriptive personality statements ("is critical, skeptical, not easily impressed") which are sorted by the assessor into nine categories, ranging from the least to the most characteristic of the person being described. Statements neither characteristic nor uncharacteristic of the individual are placed into middle categories. Each item thus receives a score from 1 to 9, and a forced symmetric distribution is employed with a mean of 5 and a standard deviation of approximately 2. The items themselves have been in use for many years and provide comprehensive coverage of the personality domain. Although not derived from any particular theoretical orientation, many of the items have a mildly psychodynamic flavor, and both phenotypic and genotypic levels of description are included. An extensive description of the Q-sort methodology in general and a detailed history of the California Q-Set in particular will be found in Block (1978).

Two Q-sorts can be compared with one another by simply computing a Pearson product-moment correlation across the items, thus expressing directly and quantitatively the degree of similarity between the two profiles. Similarly, if one has constructed a Q-sort of some hypothetical ideal personality (our "template"), one can correlate the Q-sorts of actual individuals with this idealized sort in order to assess their similarities to the ideal type. Although a Q-sort of an individual is obtained by having an assessor actually sort the 100 items into nine categories, constructing a template requires a different method for assigning numerical values to the items because only a small number of items will be relevant to any particular template. Therefore, we construct a template by "adjusting" the composite Q-sort of the entire subject sample according to the following formula:

$$Q_i = M_i + w_i\sigma_i$$

where Q_i is the adjusted or template value of the *ith* item, M_i and σ_i are the mean and standard deviation, respectively, of the *ith* item for the subject sample as a whole, and w_i is a weighting factor that reflects the "relevance" of the *ith* item to the criterion behavior being predicted.

Suppose, for example, that we are constructing a template of the hypothetical student who gets involved in too many outside activities and whose grades suffer as a result. Many of the items on the Q-set would be irrelevant, and accordingly they would be assigned weights (w_i's) of zero. The adjusted values of these items in the template, then, simply become the means of those items in the composite Q-sort of the subject sample as a whole. But consider the item "has a wide range of interests," an item that would be relevant to this template. If we assign this item a weight of, say, $+2$, then the template value of this item will be adjusted upward from the sample mean by two standard deviations, and — the model predicts — the resulting template will be more similar to the Q-sorts of students who get poor grades as a result of overin volvement in extracurricular activities than to Q-sorts of other students. A complete discussion of this template-construction algorithm will be found in Bem and Funder (1978).

Probing the Ecological Validity of the Mixed Motive Game

One of the first applications of the template-matching technique was designed by Bem and Lord (1979) to probe the ecological validity of a classical experimental setting in social psychology, the mixed motive game (the Prisoner's Dilemma Game). The question of ecological validity—Do people behave in real life as they behave in our laboratories?—is central to experimental social psychology, and the possibility that the answer might be "no" is central to the field's recent crisis of confidence (Baumrind, 1964; Orne and Holland, 1968; McGuire, 1973; Ring, 1967). Bem and Lord believed that the template matching technique might provide a novel and more direct method for assessing such validity. They selected the mixed motive game as a testing ground for the technique because the game is widely used, frequently criticized, and the debate between its proponents (such as Kelley and others, 1970) and its critics (Knox and Douglas, 1971; Nemeth, 1974; Pruitt, 1967) appears to epitomize the field's more general concern with the issue of ecological validity.

It will be recalled that in the mixed motive game, two subjects are required simultaneously to make a series of decisions independently of one another and with no communication between them. The payoff to each subject is contingent upon both of their choices. Thus in the Prisoner's Dilemma game, the most familiar of the mixed motive games, when both subjects select the "cooperative" response, their joint payoff is high; when both select the "competitive" response, their joint payoff is low; when one subject selects the cooperative response and the other the competitive response, the latter (the "defector") earns points or money at the expense of the cooperator.

Bem and Lord used the so-called "decomposed" versions of mixed motive games introduced by Messick and McClintock (1968). These games enable investigators to move beyond the simple cooperative-competitive dichotomy and to distinguish three distinct strategies of play: The J strategy in which a player attempts to maximize the *joint* gain of both players; the O strategy in which a player attempts to maximize his or her *own* absolute gain; and the R strategy in which a player attempts to maximize his or her gain *relative* to the other player. Typically it is found that individuals adopt one of these strategies consistently throughout an experiment.

Bem and Lord constructed templates for the mixed motive game situation by supplying a written description of the three strategies to five judges along with the list of Q-sort items. Each judge went through the list and gave an integer rating to each item, ranging from − 2 ("very uncharacteristic of a person following this strategy") through O ("not relevant; neither characteristic nor uncharacteristic of the person following this strategy") to + 2 ("very characteristic of the person following this strategy"). For example, the item "behaves in a giving way toward others" was given a mean rating of + 1.6 by the judges when they were characterizing the J strategy, the strategy in which players attempt to maximize the earnings of both themselves and the other player. The judges were explicitly directed not to be personality theorists, not to speculate about remote personality correlates of the behavior, but rather to judge only whether an item might or might not characterize the behavior involved in the strategy itself. The mean rating given each item by the five judges then became the weight (w_i) for that item in the template-generating algorithm described earlier. This procedure was repeated for each of the three strategies, yielding for each a template characterizing the hypothetical ideal person who pursues that strategy.

Bem and Lord recruited subjects to participate in an actual mixed motive game experiment. Q-sorts of the subjects were then obtained from their roommates, and these were correlated with each of the three templates. The results supported the ecological validity of these mixed-motive games: The subjects' Q-sorts were correlated significantly higher with the template characterizing the strategy they actually adopted in the laboratory than they were with the templates characterizing the alternative strategies. These individuals did, indeed, behave in real life as they behaved in the experimental laboratory.

Testing Competing Theories of Situations

Bem and Funder (1978) utilized the template matching technique as a vehicle for testing competing social psychological theories against one another. They, too, chose a classical experimental setting, namely, the forced compliance experiment. In such an experiment, individuals are required to advocate attitudes contrary to their own positions. The classical finding is that, subsequent to their compliance (and under theoretically specified conditions), individuals report attitudes that are closer to the advocated positions than were their initial attitudes. Several theories offer explanations for this effect. Cognitive dissonance theory, the original source of the paradigm, asserts that an aversive state of "dissonance" aroused by the discrepancy between their behavior and their contrary attitudes motivates subjects to change their attitudes (Festinger and Carlsmith, 1959). Self-perception theory (Bem, 1967, 1972) proposes that the subjects observe their own behavior of advocating the designated position and then infer their final attitudes from that behavior in much the same way that an external observer of their behavior would do. A third group of theories emphasizes the self-presentational demands of the setting and suggests that the final attitude reports given by subjects are motivated primarily by an attempt to make a particular impression on the experimenter (Tedeschi, Schlenker, and Bonoma, 1971), evaluation apprehension (Rosenberg, 1965, 1969), or a desire to project a particular "situated identity" to themselves as well as to others (Alexander and Knight, 1971).

Bem and Funder (1978) derived a separate template for each theory, a Q-sort of the hypothetical person who, according to the theory, should show the most attitude change in that situation. This was accomplished by having three judges independently select those Q-sort items that would characterize the attitude changer according to the theory. These items were then assigned weights of $+2$ or -2 (depending upon their keying) and entered into the template generating algorithm described earlier. The judges were three psychologists who have been active researcher/theoreticians in the forced compliance paradigm: A dissonance theorist (J. Merrill Carlsmith), a self-perception theorist (Daryl J. Bem), and a psychologist who has published extensively in both theories (Mark R. Lepper). The set of theories based on impression management explanations of the attitude change effect were combined by Bem and Funder into one hybrid theory called self-presentation theory.

Thirty-two college undergraduates then participated in a classical forced compliance experiment, and Q-sorts were obtained on each subject from two of his or her acquaintances. Each subject's Q-sort was correlated with the template constructed for each theory, and the template similarity scores obtained for each theory were then correlated with the attitude change scores; the higher this correlation, the better the theory is predicting attitude change. In this way, the theories were pitted against one another in predicting the individual difference variance in attitude change.

The results showed that cognitive dissonance theory was not successful at predicting attitude change, the template similarity scores actually correlating negatively with attitude change scores, $r = -.25$; self-perception theory was moderately successful, $r = .32$, $p < .10$, two-tailed. But self-presentation theory was the most successful of all, $r = .53$, $p < .005$, two-tailed.

As Bem and Funder note, the study did demonstrate that the self-presentation template accounted for more of the individual difference variance in attitude change than the other templates, but it is important not to attach too much significance to this single demonstration. In particular, some theories might be more capable of generating individual difference predictions than others, and a greater ability to predict person effects does not strictly imply a greater ability to predict situation effects. Thus Bem and Funder ran only the "choice" condition of the typical forced compliance experiment, and their contest required the theories to account for within-cell variance (person effects); conceivably their winners and losers could have fared differently in a battle over the between-cell variance (situation effects). Indeed, most social psychological theories are designed to predict treatment differences, including the theories tested in the Bem-Funder study. It was only in that study that the theories were coerced into playing the unaccustomed role of personality theories.

But this points up the real value of the template matching technique: If personological theories have not lived up to expectations because they have limited themselves to person effects in a world populated by person-situation interactions, then we should be no more hopeful about theories that limit themselves to situation effects. The template matching technique provides a potential tool for fashioning such theories into genuine theories of person-situation interaction. And, in pursuit of this promise, David Funder is currently using the template matching technique in a forced compliance experiment that requires the theories to address both within-cell and between-cell variance. In work at Cornell, David Ransen is using the template matching technique to test the possibility that different theories account for the debilitating effects of extrinsic rewards on intrinsic motivation at different ages. Similarly, Kenneth Hargis and David Maxfield at Stanford are employing the technique to explore why young children are more likely to give altruistic help when in groups rather than when alone, whereas older children and adults are more likely to help when alone (Staub, 1970). It is our hope that the template matching technique will provide a systematic way of going beyond the simple detection of interaction effects to their explanation, and hence, to begin the development of integrated theories of persons-in-situations.

The Heuristic Value of Q-Sort Information

As we have seen, the template-matching technique provides a formal mechanism for testing hypotheses about situations. But often it is the Q-sort information itself that has the most heuristic value to the investigator for revealing the functional properties of the setting and probing the meaning of the behaviors observed (Bem and Funder, 1978). For example, the Q-sort information obtained by Bem and Lord (1979) in their study of the mixed motive game provided insight into the subjects and the strategies well beyond the success of the template matching procedure. They found, for example, that the women who pursued the highly competitive R strategy in the laboratory (the strategy in which the major concern is beating the other player by the widest margin) were described by their roommates as subtly negativistic, tending to undermine, obstruct, or sabotage; keep people at a distance; avoid close interpersonal relationships; do not behave in a sympathetic or considerate manner; and so forth. In contrast, these women characterized themselves as tending to arouse liking and acceptance in people, personally charming, feminine, and having social poise and presence. Not surprisingly, their roommates rated these women signifiantly lower than they rated themselves on the item "has insight into her own motives and behavior." Note that Q-sorts provided Bem and Lord with three distinct kind of information: peer perceptions, self-perceptions, and discrepancies between the two.

The heuristic value of Q-sort information was illustrated with particular clarity in a study by Bem and Funder (1978) on the delay-of-gratification situation. As is now well known in personality psychology, behavior across seemingly similar situations is often jarringly inconsistent, rarely producing cross-situational correlations above about $+.30$ (Mischel, 1968). Moreover, it is seldom clear just what nonoverlapping features of the several situations are responsible for the observed behavioral variability across them. Bem and Funder explored the possibility that Q-sort data might provide some of this missing knowledge. They chose the classical delay-of-gratification arena for their test because there is an extensive research literature on the topic and a diversity of methods for assessing the relevant behaviors (Block and Martin, 1955; Mischel, 1974). Moreover, Mischel himself has noted that these behaviors, too, tend to be quite situation-specific (1968, p. 82).

Bem and Funder observed 29 children in an experiment that assesses how long they will wait in order to receive a preferred snack rather than a less preferred one available immediately. Q-sorts of the children were provided by their parents, using the California Child Q-set (Block and Block, 1969, Note 1). Each of the 100 items in the Q-set was then correlated with the children's delay times. As seen in Table 1, the resulting list of significantly correlated items draws a portrait of the long-delaying child in this setting.

Moreover, the positively correlated items draw a portrait of the long-delaying child which, according to Mischel, is quite consistent with the developmental literature on ego control and prosocial behavior (personal communication; see also, Mischel, 1974). Thus we see a child who, through identification ("tends to imitate and take over the characteristic manners and behavior of those he/she admires"), adopts high standards of performance, becomes protective of others, helpful, cooperative, empathic, considerate, thoughtful, and capable of develop-

Table 1. Q-Item Correlates with Delay Scores

Item	r
Positively Correlated	
Has high standards of performance for self.	.48***
Tends to imitate and take over the characteristic manners and behavior of those he/she admires.	.39**
Is protective of others.	.39**
Is helpful and cooperative.	.36*
Shows a recognition of the feelings of others, empathic.	.35*
Is considerate and thoughtful of other children.	.34*
Develops genuine and close relationships.	.31*
Negatively Correlated	
Appears to have high intellectual capacity.	− .62***
Is emotionally expressive.	− .56***
Is verbally fluent, can express ideas well in language.	− .50***
Is curious and exploring, eager to learn, open to new experiences.	− .49***
Is self-assertive.	− .47**
Is cheerful.	− .43**
Is an interesting, arresting child.	− .43**
Is creative in perception, thought, work, or play.	− .40**
Attempts to transfer blame to others.	− .37**
Behaves in a dominating way with others.	− .34*
Is restless and fidgety.	− .31*
Seeks physical contact with others.	− .31*
Is unable to delay gratification.	− .31*

After Bem and Funder (1978).

*$p < .10$ (two-tailed).
**$p < .05$ (two-tailed).
***$p < .01$ (two-tailed).

ing close relationships. Additional support for an ego control interpretation comes from some of the negatively correlated items, including, of course, the crucial item "Is unable to delay gratification." For example, the long-delaying child is seen to be emotionally unexpressive and not restless or fidgety, attributes consistent with the expressive and motoric inhibition implicated in the development of ego control (Mischel, 1966).

But the remainder of the portrait sketched in Table 1 introduces a more dissonant note, a picture of the long-delaying child as not very intelligent, not verbally fluent, not eager to learn, and not open to new experiences; a child, moreover, who is not self-assertive, cheerful, interesting or creative. The very strong negative relationship between delay and rated intelligence is particularly inconsistent with theories of ego control, and Mischel reports that he finds delay time to be positively correlated with rated intelligence in his own work (personal communication). Indeed, the gestalt that emerges from this entire set of Q-items suggests that the child who delays in this situation is as accurately described as one who is dull, passive, and obedient to adult authority as he or she is described as one who possesses a large amount of self-control.

The important point to be emphasized here is how this Q-item portrait points rather directly to the properties of the situation that appear to be salient to the children and functionally controlling. Thus it would appear that the presence of the experimenter and the implicit social desirability of delaying are as salient to the children in this setting as the differential attractiveness of the two food items, the stimulus that, on theoretical grounds, is supposed to be the controlling variable. Note how the Q-sort can function as a valuable instrument for detecting theoretically extraneous features of an experimental situation that are affecting the subjects' behaviors.

Bem and Funder then contrasted this Q-sort portrait with one that emerged from an experiment on "gift delay" by Block (1977), an experiment that is conceptually equivalent to the Bem-Funder setting. In Block's experiment, the child was shown a gaily wrapped gift and was told that it was to remain unopened until he or she completed a puzzle. The measure of "delay of gratification" was the length of time the child waited before reaching out and taking the gift. Table 2 shows the Q-items that were most highly correlated with delay in this setting.

As can be seen in Table 2, the item "is unable to delay gratification" is the best single predictor of the children's delay time. Moreover, several of the other items appear to support the interpretation that this situation is, in fact, tapping a dimension of impulse control: "planful, thinks ahead"; "attentive and able to concentrate"; "is reflective; thinks and deliberates before acting."

But it is clear that Tables 1 and 2 draw very different portraits of the long-delaying child; even the items relevant to the construct of ego control in the two tables show very little overlap, and the dull-passive-obedient cluster of items that emerged in our experiment is completely absent from the Block data. What we have here, then, are two situations that look conceptually equivalent but are functionally quite different: it would appear that different subsets of children are delaying in the two settings. As noted earlier, one typically learns only that behavior across two theoretically similar situations is disappointingly inconsistent. By collecting Q-sort data, however, one can see in exquisite detail the nature of that inconsistency and draw plausible inferences about its source in the nonoverlapping features of the settings. At the very least, Q-sort information provides valuable guidance to the investigator who needs to redesign an experimental procedure so that it serves its intended conceptual purposes. Even psychologists who

Table 2. Q-Item Correlates with Gift Delay Time
(After Block, 1977)

Item	r
Positively Correlated	
Is planful, thinks ahead.	.37
Is reflective, thinks and deliberates before acting.	.35
Becomes strongly involved in what he/she does.	.31
Is attentive and able to concentrate.	.31
Uses and responds to reason.	.30
Is shy and reserved; makes social contacts slowly.	.27
Is protective of others.	.27
Tends to keep thoughts and feelings to self.	.26
Has an active fantasy life.	.25
Negatively Correlated	
Is unable to delay gratification.	− .47
Attempts to transfer blame to others.	− .37
Has rapid shifts in mood; emotionally labile.	− .33
Is aggressive (physically or verbally).	− .32
Tries to take advantage of others.	− .31
Has transient interpersonal relationships.	− .28
Is restless and fidgety.	− .26
Emotional reactions are inappropriate.	− .26
Overreacts to minor frustrations; easily irritated.	− .26
Is stubborn.	− .25
Expresses negative feelings directly and openly.	− .25

Note: All correlations in this table are estimates based on the sex-separate correlations reported by Block (1977). I have here reproduced the 20 items with the largest estimated mean correlations.

have no particular interest in individual differences per se should welcome this entree into the phenomenology of the situations they have created.

Q-sorts not only provide information about the situations, but about the subjects as well. For example, when an experiment fails to replicate, suspicions often center upon subject sample differences, but the sparse demographic information usually available on subject samples provides little help in assessing this possibility. Composite Q-sorts of the subject samples involved would provide instant leads about possible sources of different results patterns across seemingly identical investigations. In short, it is urged that Q-sort data be routinely collected in experimental settings for several reasons — even if the investigation itself does not concern individual differences. The template matching technique is a valuable tool in the context of justification, but it is the Q-sorts themselves that excel at providing crucial information in the "context of discovery."

The Assessment of Persons

Despite the fact that the template-matching technique uses an instrument designed for the assessment of persons—the Q-sort—the technique itself is properly viewed as a way of assessing situations: A situation is defined by a set of template-behavior pairs, where the templates use the language of personality description. It has been suggested by Curt Hoffman at Stanford (personal communication) that one can apply the same technique—in reverse—to the assessment of persons. Rather than characterizing situations with templates couched in the language of personality, one would characterize persons with templates couched in the language of situations. Rather than describing a situation in terms of how a set of hypothetical ideal persons behave within it, one could describe a person in terms of how he or she behaves in a set of hypothetical ideal situations. For example, we might give an individual a set of items describing properties of situations ("is unstructured"; "encourages or demands independence"; "is characterized by the presence of an authority figure") with the instruction to construct a Q-sort or template that describes the idealized situation that makes him or her the most anxious; a second template might characterize the hypothetical situation that would evoke the most self-confidence; and so forth. One would then predict the individual's behavior in a novel situation by matching that situation's characteristics to the person's several templates and predicting that he or she would display the behavior associated with the most similar template. (A set of situational descriptors is currently under development.)

Despite the aesthetic elegance of this "symmetric" proposal, it may not be so easily executed in practice; and accordingly, Hoffman is instead currently exploring some closely related possibilities. One of these is the situationally-moderated Q-sort: First, the individual provides a standard Q-sort of him or herself (or one is obtained from a close acquaintance as we have done in our research to date). The individual is then given a situational descriptor (such as "is unstructured") and asked to indicate for each Q-sort item whether it is more or less characteristic of him or her in that kind of situation. For example, an individual might indicate that the item "is critical, skeptical, not easily impressed" is less characteristic than usual of him or her in a situation "characterized by the presence of an authority figure." This procedure is repeated for each situational descriptor. In order to predict the individual's behavior in a novel situation, one first selects the subset of situational descriptors that characterize that situation and then boosts or depresses the Q-sort items in the individual's Q-sort that, according to him or her, are moderated by those characteristics. The hypothesis is that these situationally tailored or situationally moderated Q-sorts might function significantly better in the template matching procedure than the unmoderated Q-sorts we have employed in the research we have conducted so far. More generally, each individual is characterized by not one, but a set of Q-sorts, each sort being an adjusted or situationally tailored version of his or her basic sort.

This same procedure might also enable us to identify those situations across which the individual will be consistent or inconsistent; that is, we may be able to partition situations into an individual's "equivalence classes," to identify which situations are, in fact, psychologically similar for him or her and which are not (Bem and Allen, 1974). For example, the presence or absence of an authority figure may alter several items in one individual's Q-sort—and hence, by implication, alter his or her behavior across situations differing on that characteristic—whereas another individual may be unaffected by this aspect of a situation. Current research by Charles Lord is also pursuing the problem of an individual's equivalence classes of situations; in this work the individual provides Q-sorts of *his or her conception* of persons who behave distinctively in particular situations. The hypothesis is that the similarity between an individual's conceptions of two persons (for instance, the person who is conscientious about school work and the person who is conscientious about personal appearance) is correlated with the individual's own consistency across the two pertinent contexts.

It should be clear that the research described in this section has only just begun. No data are in yet, and there is certainly no guarantee that template matching and its variants will be as successful at characterizing persons as it has been so far in characterizing situations. But at least we will have joined with other contributors to this sourcebook in trying to put some genuine substance into our shared conviction that behavior is a function of both the person and the situation.

References

Alexander, C. N., and Knight, G. W. "Situated Identities and Social Psychological Experimentation." *Sociometry*, 1971, *34*, 65–82.

Baumrind, D. "Some Thoughts on Ethics of Research: After Reading Milgram's 'Behavior Study of Obedience.'" *American Psychologist*, 1964, *19*, 421–423.

Bem, D. J. "Self-Perception: An Alternative Interpretation of Cognitive Dissonance Phenomena." *Psychological Review*, 1967, *74*, 183–200.

Bem, D. J. "Self-Perception Theory." In L. Berkowitz (Ed.), *Advances in Experimental Social Psychology*. Vol. 6. New York: Academic Press, 1972.

Bem, D. J., and Allen, A. "On Predicting Some of the People Some of the Time: The Search for Cross-Situational Consistencies in Behavior." *Psychological Review*, 1974, *81*, 506–520.

Bem, D. J., and Funder, D. C. "Predicting More of the People More of the Time: Assessing the Personality of Situations." *Psychological Review*, 1978, *85*, 485–501.

14

Bem, D. J., and Lord, C. G. "The Template-Matching Technique: A Proposal for Probing the Ecological Validity of Experimental Settings in Social Psychology." *Journal of Personality and Social Psychology*, 1979, *37*, 833–846.

Block, J. "Advancing the Psychology of Personality: Paradigmatic Shift or Improving the Quality of Research?" In D. Magnusson and N. S. Endler (Eds.), *Personality at the Crossroads: Current Issues in Interactional Psychology*. Hillsdale, N.J.: Erlbaum, 1977.

Block, J. *The Q-sort Method in Personality Assessment and Psychiatric Research*. Reprinted Edition. Palo Alto, Calif.: Consulting Psychologists Press, 1978.

Block, J., and Block, J. H. *Instructions for the California Child Q-Set*. Berkeley: Department of Psychology, University of California, 1969.

Block, J. H., and Martin, B. "Predicting the Behavior of Children Under Frustration." *Journal of Abnormal and Social Psychology*, 1955, *51*, 281–285.

Endler, N. S., and Magnusson, D. (Eds.). *Interactional Psychology and Personality*. Washington, D.C.: Hemisphere Publishing, 1976.

Festinger, L., and Carlsmith, J. M. "Cognitive Consequences of Forced Compliance." *Journal of Abnormal and Social Psychology*, 1959, *58*, 203–210.

Frederiksen, N. "Toward a Taxonomy of Situations." *American Psychologist*, 1972, *27*, 114–123.

Kelley, H. H., and others. "A Comparative Experimental Study of Negotiation Behavior." *Journal of Personality and Social Psychology*, 1970, *16*, 411–438.

Knox, R. E., and Douglas, R. L. "Trivial Incentives, Marginal Comprehension, and Dubious Generalizations from Prisoner's Dilemma Studies." *Journal of Personality and Social Psychology*, 1971, *20*, 160–165.

McGuire, W. J. "The Yin and Yang of Progress in Social Psychology: Seven Koan." *Journal of Personality and Social Psychology*, 1973, *26*, 446–456.

Magnusson, D., and Endler, N. S. (Eds.). *Personality at the Crossroads: Current Issues in Interactional Psychology*. Hillsdale, N.J.: Erlbaum, 1977.

Messick, D. M., and McClintock, C. G. "Motivational Basis of Choice in Experimental Games." *Journal of Experimental Social Psychology*, 1968, *4*, 1–25.

Mischel, W. "Theory and Research on the Antecedents of Self-Imposed Delay of Reward." In B. A. Maher (Ed.), *Progress in Experimental Personality Research*. Vol. 3. New York: Academic Press, 1966.

Mischel, W. *Personality and Assessment*. New York: Wiley, 1968.

Mischel, W. "Processes in Delay of Gratification." In L. Berkowitz (Ed.), *Advances in Experimental Social Psychology*. Vol. 7. New York: Academic Press, 1974.

Moos, R. H. "Conceptualizations of Human Environments." *American Psychologist*, 1973, *28*, 652–665.

Nemeth, C. "A Critical Analysis of Research Utilizing the Prisoner's Dilemma Paradigm for the Study of Bargaining." In L. Berkowitz (Ed.), *Advances in Experimental Social Psychology*. Vol. 6. New York: Academic Press, 1974.

Orne, M. T., and Holland, C. H. "On the Ecological Validity of Laboratory Deceptions." *International Journal of Psychiatry*, 1968, *6*, 282–293.

Pervin, L. A. "Definitions, Measurements, and Classifications of Stimuli, Situations, and Environments." *Human Ecology*, 1978, *6*, 71–105.

Pruitt, D. G. "Reward Structure and Cooperation: The Decomposed Prisoner's Dilemma Game." *Journal of Personality and Social Psychology*, 1967, *7*, 21–27.

Ring, K. "Experimental Social Psychology: Some Sober Questions about Some Frivolous Values." *Journal of Experimental Social Psychology*, 1967, *3*, 113–123.

Rosenberg, M. J. "When Dissonance Fails: On Eliminating Evaluation Apprehension from Attitude Measurement." *Journal of Personality and Social Psychology*, 1965, *1*, 18–42.

Rosenberg, M. J. "The Conditions and Consequences of Evaluation Apprehension." In R. Rosenthal and R. W. Rosnow (Eds.), *Artifacts in Behavioral Research*. New York: Academic Press, 1969.

Staub, E. "A Child in Distress: The Influence of Age and Number of Witnesses on Children's Attempts to Help." *Journal of Personality and Social Psychology*, 1970, *14*, 130–140.

Tedeschi, J. T., Schlenker, B. R., and Bonoma, T. V. "Cognitive Dissonance: Private Ratiocination or Public Spectacle?" *American Psychologist*, 1971, *26*, 685–695.

Daryl J. Bem is professor of psychology at Cornell University. Since obtaining his Ph.D. in social psychology at the University of Michigan, he has taught at Carnegie-Mellon and Stanford. He has specialized in self-perception, attitude change, and, most recently, person-situation interaction.

Making causal inferences about people and situations is now possible even without manipulating independent variables or randomly assigning research participants.

Cross-Lagged Panel Correlation and Personality

Lynn R. Kahle
John J. Berman

When picking a methodology, researchers in personality have been pulled in two opposing directions. The elegance of true experiments lures researchers toward one type of study while the advantages of correlational research enhance another. The usual inability to form causal inferences from correlational research makes the experiment attractive, but a nagging doubt nevertheless persists: Does anything about people that can be manipulated easily and ethically in fact qualify as sufficiently enduring to be called personality? In certain research circumstances, researchers may be able to reduce this conflict. In some instances it may be possible both to use correlational data, in order to study personality and how it interacts with situations, and to arrive at causal conclusions. The technique is called cross-lagged panel correlation. This method and its use in person-situation interaction research will be the focus of this chapter.

Both authors gratefully acknowledge helpful comments from Dave Kenny on cross-lagged panel correlation. Preparation of this manuscript was facilitated by NIMH Grant #MH14618.

We will begin with a set of definitions and descriptions related to this method. Then we will proceed to look at an example from person-situation interaction research. The next step will be to discuss alternative ways to use cross-lagged panel correlation in interaction research. Finally, some advantages and limitations of cross-lagged panel correlation (CLPC) are presented.

The Method

CLPC was first advocated in modern times by Campbell and Stanley (1963) and by Pelz and Andrews (1964). Kenny, Campbell, and their collaborators (Crano, Kenny, and Campbell, 1972; Kenny, 1973, 1975, 1978, 1979; Kenny and Harackiewicz, 1979; Rozelle and Campbell, 1969) have subsequently refined it.

Definitions and Basic Logic. Before going further, a few definitions will help. CLPC is a design useful for testing causal hypotheses from correlational data. *Cross-lagged* refers to the diagonal correlations in Figure 1; each is the correlation between two different variables measured at two different times (for instance, the correlation between IQ at age ten and achievement at age fifteen). *Panel* is the survey researcher's equivalent for what psychologists usually call longitudinal. A panel study measures the same subjects with the same instrument at

**Figure 1. The Six Possible First-Order Correlations
Between Two Panel Variables, A and B**

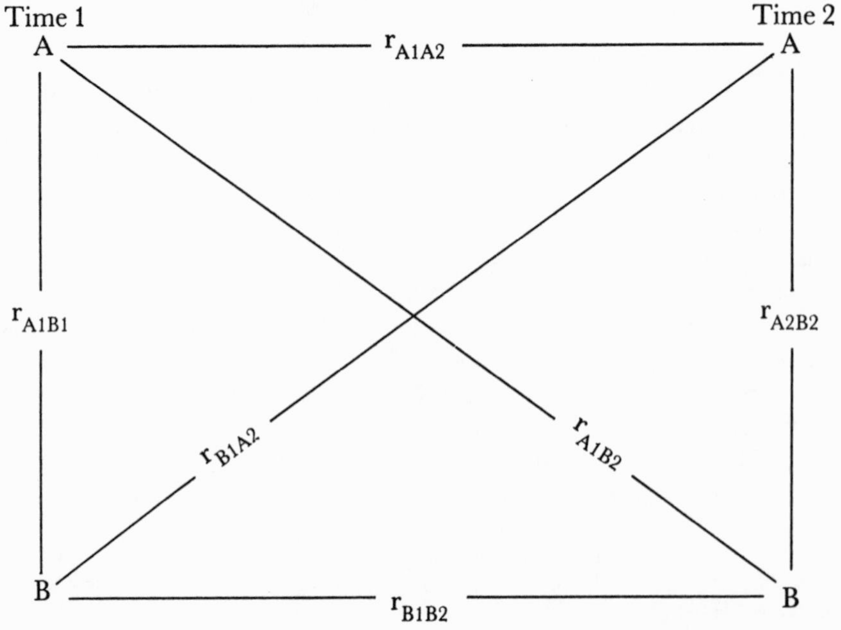

least two separate times. Within a panel study there may be both *panel variables,* which are relatively fluctuating and which are measured at more than one time, and *control variables,* which are considered very stable and, therefore, need be measured at only one point in time (for instance, sex). The term *correlation* refers to measures of the strength of the association between two variables, such as the Pearson product-moment correlation statistic.

Figure 1 presents the simplest case in which CLPC can be used. Two panel variables, A and B, have been measured at two separate times. One can compute six first-order correlations with these data, and each of these correlations is represented by one of the six lines in Figure 1. Of particular interest in this technique are the diagonal correlations, r_{A1B2} and r_{B1A2}, called the cross-lagged correlations because they criss-cross the time lag and the pair of variables. When the cross-lagged correlations differ and when various other assumptions have been satisfied, one may state that one variable has causal predominance over the other. For example, if $r_{A1B2} > r_{B1A2}$, if both are positive, and if other assumptions have been satisfied, one may state that increases in A cause increases in B, as opposed to stating either that increases in B cause increases in A or that neither variable has causal predominance over the other. The logic is as follows: An "effect" should correlate more highly with a prior "cause" than with a subsequent "cause" since causes precede effects (Campbell and Stanley, 1963, pp. 69–70).

The other two pairs of correlations pictured in Figure 1 also have names. The two correlations between A and B, r_{A1B1} and r_{A2B2}, are known as *synchronous correlations.* Synchronous literally means "same time." The correlations of each variable with itself at the other point in time, r_{A1A2} and r_{B1B2}, are known as *autocorrelations.* "Auto" literally means "self" or "same." As we shall see, both autocorrelations and synchronous correlations are important in CLPC.

Causal hypotheses predict the preponderance of causation on one variable over another variable. In CLPC the null hypothesis is that the two variables are not causally related, or, in other words, that the relationship between the two variables is spurious. The alternative hypotheses are that "A has causal preponderance over the effect B," or that "B has causal preponderance over the effect A." Since the term *cause* may offend some people's epistemological principles, the reader may wish to substitute other phrases for *causes,* such as *is functionally related to, leads to, or precedes. Cause* as used here always implies probabilistic inference and does not by any means imply metaphysically "proving" something to be "true." To say that "A causes B" is really shorthand for the statement that "something about A causes something about B" (Kenny, 1975). As Kenny (1979) employs the term, three conditions must hold before one can state that A causes B: (1) A must precede B in time. (2) A and B must be related. That is, changes in A must provide information about probable changes in B. A cannot cause B if A and B are statistically independent. (3) The relationship between A and B must be nonspurious (Suppes, 1970). Synonyms for spurious in this context are *third variable effects, common factoredness,* and *cosymptomatic effects.* If, for example, the relationship between A and B were due to variable C, then the relationship between A and B is spurious. In true experiments we use randomization to rule out the plausibility of spuriousness as an alternative explanation to experimental effects. CLPC rules out spuriousness as an alternative explanation to research effects by means of the assumptions about the data.

Assumptions. Two assumptions of CLPC are necessary to rule out spuriousness: synchronicity and stationarity. *Synchronicity* means that the processes represented in the synchronous correlations occurred at the same time, and *stationarity* means that the causal structure for the variables did not change over time.

Every statistic has assumptions. Every research procedure has assumptions. Even everyday life proceeds from assumptions. For example, when you walk into a laboratory and turn on the light switch, you assume that the electricity is flowing, that the switch works, that the light bulb filament is not burned out, and so on. CLPC has assumptions, too. Especially with innovative procedures where all of the implications of violations of assumptions are unknown, it is important to understand and heed the assumptions. On the other hand, a fear of assumptions should not terrify one so much that one refuses to flick light switches or to try new research techniques. One assumption of cross-lagged panel correlation, synchronicity, can be insured through design, and the other assumption, stationarity, is testable; hence, the assumptions are not "hopelessly implausible." (This conclusion, however, does not imply that other assumptions would not lead to other approaches, such as Cook and Campbell, 1979, as compared to Kenny and Harackiewicz, 1979.)

Although measuring the variables at the same point in time usually insures synchronicity, aggregation and retrospection can present problems for meeting this assumption (Kenny, 1975). *Aggregation* refers to variables that accumulate over time, such as Grade Point Average. *Retrospection* refers to variables that, for example, subjects may be asked to recall from the past, such as their relationship with their parents. Aggregation and retrospection may create panel variables that are not strictly synchronous. Since variables measured closer in time correlate more highly, all other things being equal, the probability that the cross-lagged correlations would differ due to a lack of synchronicity rather than a causal predominance of one variable over the other confounds the interpretation of any difference between the cross-lagged correlations.

Stationarity has to do with the structural equations of the panel variables. A structural equation, sometime called a causal equation, is the theoretical list of what makes up a variable, just as the "Ingredients" list in a recipe is a list of what makes up a stew. More specifically, a structural equation expresses the relative contribution of each cause of a variable. Stationarity may be of at least two types: perfect stationarity or quasi-stationarity. When the structural equation of the panel variable does not change over time (that is, when the contribution of each cause remains the same), perfect stationarity is obtained. A lack of change in synchronous correlations is consistent with perfect stationarity. Measuring a variable in the same manner at each time, however, does not insure that one will obtain perfect stationarity.

Quasi-stationarity refers to the case where the structural equation of each variable changes over time by a constant unique for each variable (Kenny, 1975). The implication of the assumption of quasi-stationarity is that the synchronous correlations would equal each other if corrected for attenuation due to measurement unreliability. If a set of data meets the assumptions of quasi-stationarity but not perfect stationarity, it is necessary to adjust the cross-lagged correlations prior to testing for spuriousness. This adjustment is necessary because variables with decreasing reliability would otherwise appear to be causes and variables with increasing reliability would appear to be effects. This correction may be employed only when sample size is over 100.

Researchers can test the various assumptions of stationarity statistically (Kenny, 1973, 1975, 1978) when they have several panel variables. With at least three panel variables one may test the assumptions of perfect stationarity and may adjust the synchronous and cross-lagged correlations in an attempt to meet the assumptions of quasi-stationarity. With at least four panel variables one may also test the assumptions of quasi-stationarity. If a set of data fails to meet the test of quasi-stationarity, CLPC is an inappropriate technique. The researcher confronted with a lack of quasi-stationarity should consider abandoning some of the panel variables that are least stationary or should consider using a different statistical technique. Kenny (1978) has produced a Fortran computer program, PANAL, for testing or correcting panel data for stationarity. This program is extremely valuable in CLPC analyses.

CLPC has other assumptions and limitations, which we shall mention below, but synchronicity and stationarity are the most critical since Kenny (1973) has provided the mathematical model that, given stationarity, synchronicity, and spuriousness, the cross-lagged correlations do not differ. Thus, when the assumptions of synchronicity and stationarity are justified, we can test the null hypothesis of no causal relationship.

A Research Example

At this point it will be valuable to look at a detailed example of the use of CLPC in person-situation interactions. A brief theoretical interlude will first be necessary, however.

Stimulus Condition Self-Selection. How do situations and persons interact? This question may well be the most important one facing researchers in personality today. One partial answer to it is that certain types of people select certain types of situations or stimulus conditions that are consistent with their personality. Although many theorists have proposed a version of this idea (Mischel, 1976, pp. 510–511; Wachtel, 1973, p. 330), it has defied rigorous empirical investigation because allowing people to select and/or modify their stimulus conditions defied the research tradition of random assignment to stimulus conditions.

Consider the following example: A researcher wants to study whether traits or situations are the better predictors of behavior. He or she identifies a population of book worms indifferent to football and a population of football fans indifferent to books. Representatives of each population are randomly assigned either to a library or to a football game. The researcher discovers that, independent of the type of person, subjects at the football game watch football and subjects in the library read. Our researcher infers, therefore, that traits and behavior are unrelated and that situations have more predictive utility with respect to reading and watching football than do traits. If our researcher had allowed the book worms and the football fans to select their own stimulus conditions, however, the inferences may have differed. Football fans would probably stream toward the stadium while book worms would snake toward the library. But our researcher would not allow such events to occur because the independent variables would have been unmanipulated and the inferences therefore weakened.

Here is a research question where a true experiment is not really appropriate but where CLPC analysis could be useful. An attempt was made here to answer the questions of whether people self-select stimulus conditions consistent with the type of person they are and whether the selections relate to behaviors. Specifically, the hypotheses were that attitudes lead to stimulus condition self-selections and that stimulus condition self-selections lead to behaviors.

Method. Over 300 introductory psychology students participated in the research by completing questionnaires on four issues — Jimmy Carter's presidential candidacy, Gerald Ford's candidacy, drinking, and religion—each measured at two points in time. The times of measurement were just after the Republican Party had selected Ford as its nominee and again two months later, just prior to the 1976 presidential elections. (We will omit some of the technical detail irrelevant to cross-lagged panel correlation since it has been reported in Kahle (1977) and in Kahle and Berman (1979).

The first task was to develop reliable measures of the constructs. This was done by pilot tests and extensive statistical analyses of the internal consistency of these pilot data. Items that reduced the internal consistency of scales were discarded. Such careful attention to establishing reliable measures is probably even more important in CLPC research than it is in other types of investigations. For the group of subjects used in the cross-lagged analyses the median Cronbach's alpha for the various constructs was .83. These are relatively high values and indicate that the items constituting each scale were for the most part measuring the same thing. Examples of the items used are presented in Table 1. At both points in time subjects rated each attitude item on a scale ranging from *strongly agree* (= 1) to *strongly disagree* (= 9). For the stimulus condition self-selection items and for the behavior items, sub-

Table 1. Representative Items from Each Set of Questions

Carter Issues
Attitude: I strongly support Jimmy Carter for president.
Stimulus Condition Self-selection: How many times in the past 14 days have you decided to hear a political speech favorable to Jimmy Carter?
Behavior: How many times in the past 14 days have you made a favorable comment about Jimmy Carter?

Ford Issues
Attitude: I strongly support Gerald Ford for president.
Stimulus Condition Self-selection: How many times in the past 14 days have you decided to hear a political speech favorable to Gerald Ford?
Behavior: How many times in the past 14 days have you made a favorable comment about Gerald Ford?

Drinking Issues
Attitude: I like to drink.
Stimulus Condition Self-selection: How many times in the past 14 days have you gone to a place to get alcoholic beverages?
Behavior: How many times in the past 14 days have you had at least 1 drink?

Religion Issues
Attitude: Being active in church is important.
Stimulus Condition Self-selection: How many times in the past 14 days have you gone to a place where you expected to discuss religion? How many times in the past 14 days have you sought out people from your church?
Behavior: How many times in the past 14 days have you prayed in private? How many times in the past 14 days have you been with people from your church?

---

jects were asked how many times in the past 14 days they had engaged in the activity mentioned in the item. They also rated a number of control variables. Since the control variables were continuously measured and were expected to be stable over the time period studied, they were partialed from the panel variables.

The time-lag was selected to be appropriate for the political issues, and it may or may not have been appropriate for the drinking and religion issues. Ideally, one should select a time lag during which one expects a moderate amount of change. A great deal of change among the subjects is probably associated with a lack of stationarity. Little or no change does not allow for the detection of casual influences.

Preliminary Results. Before one knows whether it is even meaningful to look at any differences in the cross-lagged correlations, it is important to examine several other aspects of the data. The first step is to examine the autocorrelations. One wants these correlations to be positive and moderately high. Autocorrelations that are too high imply too little change for detecting causation, and autocorrelations too low imply a lack of stationarity. The results showed that these autocorrelations were of the desired magnitude since the values ranged from .28 to .77. The next step is to inspect the synchronous correlations. They should also be moderately high because low synchronous correlations imply that no relationship exists between the variables to be explained and very high correlations imply that the two scales are measuring the same construct. The synchronous correlations between attitudes and stimulus condition self-selections were all positive and moderate with a median of .46. The correlations of stimulus condition self-selection with behavior for the Carter and Ford data were .63 and .69, respectively, which presents no problem. These correlations in the religion and drinking data, however, were .79 and .81. In these two cases the two constructs probably shared considerable method variance. This result is not too surprising since stimulus condition self-selection is itself a type of behavior, but such a result yields a set of cross-lagged correlations that are more difficult to interpret. In other research we have established that the two constructs differ (Kahle, in press), but in the present research only the political data will give meaningful information about the second hypothesis.

The synchronous correlations also give information about the important assumption of stationarity. Equal synchronous correlations indicate perfect stationarity. To check this assumption, we tested the equality of the synchronous correlations, using the Pearson-Filon test for differences between correlated correlations (see Kenny, 1975, for the formula). If the synchronous correlations statistically equal each other, then we can proceed to test the difference between the raw cross-lagged correlations with the Pearson-Filon test. Such was the case for the drinking and religion issues.

Since some synchronous correlations were not equal, we then calculated "reliability ratios" (Kenny, 1975, p. 897; Kenny, 1978). These are first used to test the assumption of quasi-stationarity, which implies that the synchronous correlations would be equal if corrected for measurement error. If this assumption is not tenable, the differences between the crosslags cannot be interpreted. Remember that we need at least four panel variables in order to test the quasi-stationarity assumption. Because we cannot count on obtaining perfect stationarity and, therefore, would always want to be able to test for quasi-stationarity, one should not plan a CLPC analysis with fewer than four panel variables. According to the output from PANAL, the computer program for these analyses (Kenny, 1978), the variables concerning Carter and Ford were consistent with the assumption of quasi-stationarity, although the results indicated that a slight amount of caution is called for in interpreting the Ford data because the weights used for the correction (Kenny, 1978) were somewhat small.

Cross-Lagged Results. Table 2 displays the cross-lagged correlations and the results from the Pearson-Filon test. The degrees of freedom for the tests are N–2: 360 for the political data, 392 for the religion data, and 324 for the drinking data.

What do these data tell us about stimulus condition self-selection? It appears that person factors such as attitudes do lead to stimulus

Table 2. Tests of the Hypotheses that Attitudes (a) Lead to ($\rightarrow$) Stimulus Condition Self-Selections (S) and that Stimulus Condition Self-Selections Lead to Behaviors (B)

Issues	HL	HS	z
Carter Issues			
A→S	.48	.18	5.20**
S→B	.46	.27	3.55**
Ford Issues			
A→S	.22	.10	1.75*
S→B	.34	.21	2.45**
Religion Issues			
A→S	.49	.40	1.95*
S→B	.61	.67	– 1.83*
Drinking Issues			
A→S	.54	.49	1.20
S→B	.63	.65	– 0.67

*p<.1
**p<.05

Note: HL refers to the cross-lagged correlations that were Hypothesized to be Larger (i.e., r_{A1S2} and r_{S1B2}). HS refers to the cross-lagged correlations that were Hypothesized to be Smaller (i.e., r_{A2S1} and r_{S2B1}). z refers to the Pearson-Filon Test for the significance of differences between correlated correlations (Kenny, 1975).

condition self-selections. On three of the four issues attitudes did lead to stimulus condition self-selections, and on the remaining issue the cross-lagged correlation difference was at least in the hypothesized direction. Since the cross-lagged difference was not significant for either hypothesis in the drinking data, it would probably be advisable to test different time lags before completely embracing the null hypothesis. The hypothesis that "stimulus conditions cause behaviors" obtained strong support in the Carter data and in the more questionable Ford data. In the religion and drinking data, where the synchronous correlations suggested considerable shared method variance, the cross-lagged correlation difference is in the opposite direction of the hypothesis, significantly so in the case of the religion data. Although other research we have done (Kahle, in press) tends to give us confidence in the second hypothesis, the present religion and drinking data with their very large synchronous correlations confuse the issue more than clarify it.

This line of research is still in progress, and any final conclusions are premature. But the early evidence is exciting. A number of writers have noted that within situations the correlations between person variables, such as attitudes and traits, and behaviors tend to be quite low. Mischel (1968) coined the term "personality coefficient" to describe the correlations of .30 found so frequently between person variables and behaviors within situations. These low correlations have created some pessimism about the utility of person variables. If person variables influence behaviors in part through the selection of situations, however, then correlations that reflect only behavior within situations will tend to be spuriously low. By understanding the processes by which person-situation interactions occur, we may come to a greater appreciation of the importance of both types of variables. In his provocative and fascinating essay, Ross (1977) identified the "fundamental attribution error," as discovered from laboratory research. It is that lay attributors pay too little attention to situations in laboratory research. By ignoring stimulus condition self-selection, attributionists may have erred in this inference. Insufficient attention to the importance of stimulus condition self-selection may be the fundamental attributionist error.

Using Information About Persons and About Situations in CLPC Research

Perhaps the most immediately obvious way in which cross-lagged panel correlation could help illuminate person-situation interactions would be to have two types of panel variables — those measuring persons and those measuring exposure to situations. In such a case we would have to pay particular attention to the assumption of Pearsonian correlations that both the personality variable and the situation variable are continuous (interval scales). This assumption may not always be valid, especially with regard to situation variables. Furthermore, although the basic unit of analysis in cross-lagged panel correlation consists of only two panel variables, the results of only one such unit of analysis in isolation would rarely be interesting. One reason is that this analysis would not provide any information about stationarity. In addition, the question answered by such a comparison — does the situation here cause the trait or vice versa — may often be too simplistic to be informative.

One method for increasing the interest level of such analyses would be to sample multiple time lags. With multiple time lags it may be possible to obtain information about reciprocal causation or cyclical causation. The replication of any obtained effects adds strength to any conclusions even in the absence of reciprocal or cyclical causation. And when one is initially unsure about the proper time lag, the sampling of multiple time lags may help to establish just what the correct time lag is. Calsyn (1973) provided one of the best-designed examples of the use of cross-lagged panel correlation in personality research when he attempted to show that academic achievement has causal predominance over academic self-concept. In that study he not only sampled multiple time lags, but he also used multiple methods of assessing the same construct and multiple subject populations. Such a thorough methodology comes much closer to the concept of interaction than would a study that involved only two measurement times.

Another way to approach the concept of interaction is through the use of control variables, also called background variables. As defined above, control variables are measured only once because they are unlikely to change during the time lag. Kenny (1975) proposed that control variables should only be selected when they can explain a moderate amount of variance. Also, it makes sense that any control variable should in principle explain approximately as much of the variance of the Time 1 variables as of the Time 2 variables. Kahle and Berman (1979) also propose that a control variable should have at least some theoretical importance.

One approach to control variables is to do separate analyses for each level of the control variable (assuming that sample size is sufficiently large). This procedure would be appropriate where one expected contrasting patterns of causation. For example, if one expected that a certain trait causes interesting behaviors only in some situations, one might measure the trait and behaviors in several types of situations, compute cross-lagged analyses separately on the data from each situation, and then compare the sets of results. Likewise, one could compare different types of people to see if the causal relationship between situations and behaviors or other traits is the same for each type. Crano, Kenny, and Campbell (1972), for example, found that intelligence tends to be causally predominant over achievement for middle class children but not for lower class children.

The other method for dealing with control variables is to remove the effect of the control variables from all of the panel variables with partial correlation. The analysis of the cross-lagged correlations is then performed on partial correlations. This procedure would be appropriate where control variables increased the stationarity of the panel variables. Often one may want to study only a set of personality variables or only a set of situational variables, even though one is fully aware that both people and situations are important. In this case it would be wise to take into account the variables of less interest by partialling out their effects. Or more generally, one may often be interested in certain variables while recognizing that a number of others, both person and situation variables, are important to those variables of primary concern. Partial correlation may again be the appropriate method for dealing with the variables of secondary interest. Although partial correlation may in some cases be controversial (Brewer, Campbell, and Crano, 1970), it is appropriate when the control variables are stable.

Yet another way to use CLPC within the context of person-situation interactions is to design panel variables specifically for testing hypotheses related to issues raised by the concepts involved with person-situation interactions. The procedure is not mutually exclusive from the other procedures. Thus far, theorizing about person-situation interactions has proceeded at a much faster pace than has the gathering of empirical evidence to support or refute the theorizing. A number of specific hypotheses about interactions remain to be tested, and many of these hypotheses could be tested through the use of CLPC.

Advantages and Limitations of CLPC

CLPC has an obvious advantage over traditional correlations in that it can be used for causal inferences. It also has some advantages over traditional experimental designs since randomization and variable manipulation are not necessary assumptions of it. As a correlational design, it has the further advantage that one need not discriminate between independent and dependent variables a priori. This fact is important because Bowers (1973) has criticized the experimental approach (in the sense of "true" experiments where subjects are assigned randomly to conditions) to the study of personality as being based on social learning assumptions. Independent variables (stimuli and situations) will lead to changes in dependent variables (responses and behaviors), making it impossible to falsify the social learning approach, unless one accepts null hypotheses. The independent-dependent variable relationship in experiments is too directly analogous to the stimulus-response relationship. Stimuli never become dependent variables in these designs. Such criticism does not apply to cross-lagged analyses where one could in principle falsify social learning hypotheses. In the attitude-behavior controversy, for example, both attitudes and behaviors could have equal probability of showing up as a cause or an effect in a CLPC design (Kahle and Berman, 1979). Furthermore, correlational studies often have better external validity than laboratory studies (Page and Kahle, 1976).

Although CLPC has several advantages over experimental designs, it also has several limitations or weaknesses in comparison to them. The first limitation is that CLPC is a low power statistical procedure. The most common method for overcoming a lack of statistical power is to increase the sample size. Kenny (1975) notes that even a sample size of 300 may be too small in some instances. It would not often be worthwhile to compute cross-lagged panel correlations with fewer than 200 subjects.

We recommend that one should be skeptical of cross-lagged correlation significance tests when the larger cross-lagged correlation (in terms of absolute value) has a different sign (+ or −) than the synchronous correlations (which should always have the same sign). When the cross-lagged correlations have different signs (+ or −), then researchers should also establish that the absolute values of the cross-lagged correlations differ. For example, Rozelle and Campbell (1969) studied the relationship between class attendance and grades. They found that the correlation between $attendance_1$ and $grades_2$ was larger than the correlation between $grades_1$ and $attendance_2$, .081 > − 063. Since the absolute value of these correlations is nearly the same, the significant difference between the two may indicate that high attendance causes high grades, that high grades cause low attendance, or that no causation exists at all.

Another problem with CLPC (as well as with all empirical research) is specifying the appropriate time lag. Nothing about cross-lagged panel correlation specifies what the appropriate time lag might be with respect to a particular research question. Quite often social science theory also fails to guide researchers to an appropriate time lag. This problem also exists in other longitudinal research and in laboratory research. In the area of attitude change, for example, McGuire (1960) argued that laboratory cognitive consistency manipulations may not show their full effect for a week. The time lag for change in the absence of experimental manipulation is probably often much longer.

One possible solution to this problem would be to sample numerous time lags.

CLPC, as is true of other research techniques, yields more interpretable results when the measures used are reliable, valid, and unitary. Researchers should take great care in selecting and pilot testing their measures. Since increased reliability augments power, reliability is very important in CLPC. Although in one sense the autocorrelations provide an index of the reliability of measures, stability (test-retest) reliability may not be the most desirable index when studying change (Carver, 1974; Kenny, 1975). In a pretest-postest laboratory study of personality, for example, it would be neither helpful nor desirable for the test-retest reliability within the experimental group to be extremely high. Such stability might overly inflate the probability that one would not reject the null hypothesis when the null hypothesis was in fact false. More useful gauges of reliability in cross-lagged panel data are measures of internal consistency such as Cronbach's alpha. Ideally, researchers would want highly reliable variables that, nevertheless, were changing (as indicated by moderate autocorrelations).

Missing data can also be an issue in the computation of longitudinal correlations. Pair-wise deletion, or deleting only subjects for whom data are missing for the pair of panel variables that one is correlating at the moment, presents a problem. One almost always wants to examine several panel variables at once, but the samples for the correlations between the various pairs could then differ. For CLPC studies, Kenny (1975) advocates list-wise deletion in which all correlations are computed only for subjects for whom one has complete data on all variables within a particular analysis. List-wise deletion, of course, reduces sample size. Although in some types of research such subject attrition could introduce a bias, Kenny (1975) has pointed out that subject attrition may not bias correlations to the extent that it can bias means. Nevertheless, researchers should explain any large reduction in sample-size when this happens.

Conclusion

Cross-lagged panel correlation is no longer a methodological mutant nor an unworkable set of impossible assumptions. The time has come when it should be taught and used as an important tool in personality research and person-situation interaction research. It allows researchers to ask important questions about personality that have never before been asked or answered. It is neither a panacea nor a simple method, but it is a worthwhile approach to employ when studying person-situation interactions.

References

Bowers, K. S. "Situationism in Psychology: An Analysis and a Critique." *Psychological Review,* 1973, *80,* 307–336.

Brewer, M., Campbell, D. T., and Crano, W. "The Use of Partial Correlations to Test Hypotheses." *Sociometry,* 1970, *33,* 1–11.

Calsyn, R. J. "The Causal Relationship between Self-Esteem, Locus of Control, and Achievement: A Cross-Lagged Panel Analysis." Unpublished doctoral dissertation, Northwestern University, 1973.

Campbell, D. T., and Stanley, J. C. *Experimental and Quasi-Experimental Designs for Research.* Chicago: Rand McNally, 1963.

Carver, R. P. "Two Dimensions of Tests." *American Psychologist,* 1974, *29,* 512–518.

Cook, T. D., and Campbell, D. T. *Quasi-Experimentation: Design and Analysis Issues for Field Settings.* Chicago: Rand McNally, 1979.

Crano, W. D., Kenny, D. A., and Campbell, D. T. "Does Intelligence Cause Achievement? A Cross-Lagged Panel Analysis." *Journal of Educational Psychology,* 1972, *63,* 258–275.

Kahle, L. R. "Stimulus Condition Self-Selection in Person-Situation Interactionism." Unpublished doctoral dissertation, University of Nebraska, Lincoln, 1977.

Kahle, L. R. "Stimulus Condition Self-Selection by Males in the Interaction of Locus of Control and Skill-Chance Situations." *Journal of Personality and Social Psychology,* in press.

Kahle, L. R., and Berman, J. J. "Attitudes Cause Behaviors: A Cross-Lagged Panel Analysis." *Journal of Personality and Social Psychology,* 1979, *37,* 315–321.

Kenny, D. A. "Cross-Lagged Synchronous and Common Factors in Panel Data." In A. S. Goldberger and O. D. Duncan (Eds.), *Structural Equation Models in the Social Sciences.* New York: Seminar Press, 1973.

Kenny, D. A. "Cross-Lagged Panel Correlation: A Test for Spuriousness." *Psychological Bulletin,* 1975, *82,* 887–903.

Kenny, D. A. *PANAL: A Computer Program for Panel Data Analysis.* Storrs: Department of Psychology Research Report, University of Connecticut, 1978.

Kenny, D. A. *Correlation and Causality.* New York: Wiley, 1979.

Kenny, D. A., and Harackiewicz, J. M. "Cross-Lagged Panel Correlation: Practice and Promise." *Journal of Applied Psychology,* 1979, *64,* 372–379.

McGuire, W. J. "Cognitive Consistency and Attitude Change." *Journal of Abnormal and Social Psychology,* 1960, *60,* 345–353.

Mischel, W. *Personality and Assessment.* New York: Wiley, 1968.

Mischel, W. *Introduction to Personality.* (2nd ed.). New York: Holt, Rinehart and Winston, 1976.

Page, M. M., and Kahle, L. R. "Demand Characteristics in the Satiation-Deprivation Effect on Attitude Conditioning." *Journal of Personality and Social Psychology,* 1976, *33,* 553–562.

Pelz, D. C., and Andrews, F. M. "Detecting Causal Priorities in Panel Study Data." *American Sociological Review,* 1964, *29,* 836–848.

Ross, L. "The Intuitive Psychologist and His Shortcomings: Distortions in the Attribution Process." In L. Berkowitz (Ed.), *Advances in Experimental Social Psychology.* Vol. 10. New York: Academic Press, 1977.

Rozelle, R. M., and Campbell, D. T. "More Plausible Rival Hypotheses in the Cross-Lagged Panel Correlation Technique." *Psychological Bulletin,* 1969, *71,* 74–80.

Suppes, P. *A Probabilistic Theory of Causality.* Amsterdam: North Holland Publishing, 1970.

Wachtel, P. "Psychodynamics, Behavior Therapy, and the Implacable Experimenter: An Inquiry into the Consistency of Personality." *Journal of Abnormal Psychology,* 1973, *82,* 324–338.

Lynn R. Kahle is a postdoctoral fellow at the Institute for Social Research, University of Michigan.

John J. Berman is an associate professor of social psychology at the University of Nebraska, Lincoln.

Modern social psychology is rich in theory and richer
still in small facts. But firm knowledge about close and
lasting relationships, built on careful study of those
relationships as they develop, settle into stable forms,
and sometimes dissolve, is rarely to be seen.

Assessing Interpersonal Relationships in Natural Settings

Donald R. Peterson

Over twenty-five years of research and practice in clinical psychology, I have become increasingly convinced that most human misery and mental derangement are tied to the things people do with each other in their interpersonal relationships. The greatest joys and satisfactions of human experience seem just as surely to come through the relationships people have with one another. As a practicing clinician, I must deal with the twisted communications of husbands and wives, the subtle authority maneuvers of parents and their children, with loneliness, anger, love and its loss, feelings of control and being controlled, the balance of doing for others and taking care of oneself. None of these is an isolated "personality" problem. All are rooted in the relationships between the person who "has" the problem and other people who matter in his life or hers. The person interacts with the human components in the surrounding situation.

The research discussed in this chapter was done at the University of Illinois and at Rutgers University with support from the National Institute of Mental Health, the University of Illinois Research Board, and the Grant Foundation.

There is no shortage of treatment techniques for people with interpersonal problems. The variety of family therapies available these days is nearly as amazing as the array of encounter group methods so popular ten years ago. For me as a clinician, the main problem is to figure out what is wrong with the relationship in the first place. Only then can ways of helping people be intelligently fashioned. The most troublesome issues I face in clinical practice have more to do with assessment than treatment, and with few exceptions currently available methods for the assessment of interpersonal disorders are either inappropriate or unreliable.

As a researcher in social psychology, I am equally frustrated by the lack of good methods for studying interpersonal relationships. I am especially concerned about the lack of powerful methods for studying interpersonal *process,* in *close* relationships, in *natural* settings. The social psychology of our time is mainly a psychology of casual relationships studied under artificial conditions. Two college sophomores are placed in a laboratory somewhere and asked to resolve a conflict or play some other experimental game. By the time enough of them have done that, enough others have played some carefully controlled variant of the game, and elaborate statistical analyses have wrung the data dry of information, something may be learned of the way college sophomores treat each other in the laboratory rooms of psychology buildings. But nothing more will be known about the slow deterioration of marriages or the drifting of sons and daughters away from their parents. Modern social psychology is rich in theory and richer still in small facts. But firm knowledge about close and lasting relationships, built on careful study of those relationships as they develop, settle into stable forms, and sometimes dissolve, is rarely to be seen.

A Plan for Studying Close Relationships

In an earlier statement (Peterson, 1968) an effort was made to define the kind of methodology psychologists will have to create in order to develop useful, dependable knowledge about the natural processes of social behavior. The scope of the first statement was very broad. It dealt with the study of individual behavior in situational context, social behavior in primary groups, and functional activities in organizations. A later statement (Peterson, 1977) narrowed consideration to interpersonal relationships and proposed a research plan for constructing and evaluating needed methods for the study of interaction process. In both statements a methodology is considered likely to yield dependable, useful information to the extent that the following conditions are met:

1. The subject of inquiry is the interaction of person with situation. This idea sounds platitudinous today, but more than ten years after the "case for the situation" was made by Sells (1963), Endler and Hunt (1966), Mischel (1968), and others, it is still true that the vast majority of instruments for studying human behavior do not deal with interactional units. They deal with the person alone, in the case of personality measures, or the situation alone, in the case of experimental procedures. For interpersonal relationships, the dominant features of situations are other people. We deal with person-person interactions.

2. Inquiries are directed toward processes over time, rather than toward states, traits, or any other conditions examined at a single time. This requires study of the sequential relationships among behavioral events, the antecedents of the events, and the consequences of the events. As one corollary of this condition, no traditional test, no "snapshot" device for the study of psychological characteristics — neither Rorschach, MMPI, locus of control scale, rating of interpersonal attraction, static index of aggression, nor any test resembling any of those measures — can alone yield useful information for the study of psychological process. This is true in principle, not merely in fact.

3. Characterizations of psychological process represent significant natural events as these occur in their natural settings. Indeterminacy prevails in all sciences, but conditions of indeterminacy pose especially severe problems for psychology because human beings are much more reactive to observation than most other organisms or physical objects appear to be. The more contrived and artificial the conditions of investigation are, the less likely are valid representations of significant natural process to emerge from the investigation. It is exactly those "valid representations of significant natural process" that useful psychological inquiry must provide.

4. The formulations of interaction process include covert as well as overt aspects of behavior. Full understanding of significant human interaction is at least very difficult and in some regards impossible without considering the covert activities of the participants as well as their explicitly observable behavior. If this condition is accepted, observation alone becomes an insufficient method for studying interpersonal relationships.

5. Methods for the study of interaction process are multimodal in character. No single test, no single operation of any kind is likely to provide information about the many facets of interpersonal process required for comprehensive knowledge about the process. Instead, a full range of the methods of behavioral science, namely, observations and records of behavior, verbal inquiry, elicitative procedures, and the experimental management of behavior may all be usefully employed.

6. Methods of inquiry, and the characterizations they are designed to provide, are defined within a reasonably coherent conception of human behavior. There is no such thing as free empiricism in science. All inquiries are guided by some conception, implicit or explicit, that leads the investigator to examine some phenomena rather than others and to frame descriptions of those phenomena in one set of terms instead of another. Since that is the case, it is reasonable to propose that the conceptions guiding any inquiry be stated as clearly as possible as the inquiry begins and then restated as the facts of inquiry suggest.

7. Methods of studying psychological process satisfy at least minimal conditions of psychometric dependability. Most fundamentally, this requires that any descriptive proposition to emerge from an examination be capable of intersubjective test and that appropriate tests show reasonable levels of agreement.

As far as I know, no body of research based on methods that meet all of the preceding conditions can be found in social psychology today. And research to develop the needed methods is inherently slow-moving. I have been actively involved in such inquiries for eight years now. Two years were spent in planning, four years in data collection, and two years in analyzing data from just one of the procedures. Method development for the study of interpersonal process is no place for anybody who needs to publish a great many articles in a hurry. Although our analyses have only begun, there may be some value in describing the general features of the research program and in showing the kinds of information we have gotten from one of the more promising methods to come from the work.

The conception of interpersonal process about which our inquiries are organized starts with definition of the *interaction sequence* as a unit of exchange. An interaction sequence begins when an act by one person is followed by contingent action on the part of another, continues as long as mutual contingency prevails in the ensuing interaction, and ends when mutual contingency between the actions of participants ceases. I go to see my barber for a haircut. We greet each other, I sit down, he cuts my hair as we talk about fishing or the weather or whatever moves us that day, he asks me if I am satisfied with the job he did, I tell him I am, get up and pay him, he thanks me, and we say goodbye. My wife and I come downstairs for breakfast in the morning. I make the coffee while she slices a cantaloupe. In other ways we work together to get breakfast on the table. We talk of our plans for the day, and maybe listen to some music or watch the birds at the feeder as the meal proceeds. In time we finish eating and clear the dishes together. I get my briefcase and put on my coat, we embrace, in one way or another show our fondness for one another, and I am off for work.

Those are interaction sequences, the basic materials of which relationships are made.

In close, lasting relationships certain patterns of interaction tend to recur with only minor variations from one sequence to the next. Except for the food, one dinnertime routine is much like another. The fight patterns of resentful husbands and wives become wearily predictable. Both parties know when they are in for a battle, fight it out in full furor, gasp and wipe up the damage when they are done, and yet know as they do so that they have been through it all many times before. At any stage in the course of a relationship, the pattern of recurrent interactions that takes place between the participants *is* the relationship. When the interaction pattern changes, the relationship has changed.

The design of procedures for studying interaction sequences requires some decisions about the aspects of each interaction to examine. Shall we record only externally observable behavior, or shall we also try to determine what the participants are thinking and feeling? Of all the explicit behavior on display, which shall we study most closely? Shall we try to register every twitch, or will the study of more molar actions lead to clearer regularities? If we elect to study covert processes, how far shall we go with our inferences? In the provisional conception about which we started out inquiries at the University of Illinois (Peterson, 1977), five main aspects of any interaction were identified. These were the *setting conditions* under which the interaction occurred, the *normative rules* establishing the rights and obligations of the participants, the *interpersonal strategies* people employed in their efforts to gain satisfactory outcomes, the *interpersonal tactics,* especially the verbal and nonverbal communications people expressed through the process of interaction, and the *reward-cost outcomes* accruing to each party by the end of the sequence. At the time, our plans were strongly influenced by exchange conceptions of social behavior (Carson, 1969; Homans, 1961; Thibaut and Kelley, 1959). Some of the features of exchange that seemed worth examining at that earlier stage still seem important now. Even the partial data we have analyzed so far, however, suggest different emphases, and the conception of interpersonal process derived from the data is different in several ways from the conception with which we began. The revised view will become clear in the material to follow.

In keeping with the idea that a wide range of methods should be employed in studying any phenomena as complex as interpersonal relationships, an extensive set of procedures was developed. These included guided interviews, *in situ* observations, detailed records kept by the participants, a battery of questionnaires, and several analog procedures, including Strodtbeck's Revealed Differences Method (Strodtbeck, 1951), some improvisations as used by Raush and others (1974), and re-enactments of actual conflicts the participants reported. Studies so far have all been done with married couples, some of whom said their marriages were happy, some of whom were seeking clinical help to deal with marital problems, and some of whom said nothing special about the quality of their marriages. Our continuing intent has been to examine data within each of these modes separately, to determine the basic psychometric properties of each procedure as we go, and to see what conceptions of interpersonal process seem to fit the facts best as data flow from the various approaches we have taken. Then we can study convergences among methods. In some version of a multitrait-multimethod design (Campbell and Fiske, 1959), we can determine whether interaction process as viewed by one procedure bears any resemblance to the process as seen by other methods. Finally, we can see what kind of general conception can be framed to fit all the information we have obtained. The whole inquiry is predominantly inductive. It is therefore indefinite and lengthy. I am beginning to wish I had paid more attention to my age when I began the project.

So far, detailed analyses have only been completed for one of the methods, namely interaction records couples were asked to keep during the week between testing sessions (Peterson, 1978). The remainder of this chapter will be devoted mainly to that method, to some information we have gained from its use, and to the conception of interaction process that developed as we attempted to make sense of the detailed accounts of interpersonal experience these people brought to us.

Procedure for Obtaining Interaction Records

At the end of each day husbands and wives were to sit down together, discuss the things that had gone on between them that day, and decide on the most important interaction they had had. We told them what we meant by an interaction, but let them determine which interactions were "important" for them. Then, on a form we provided, they were to write independent accounts of the interactions from start to finish. The forms asked them to indicate: (1) *the conditions under which the interaction took place* (Where and when did it happen? How were you both feeling as the interaction began? Were there any previous events which influenced what happened between you?); (2) *how the interaction started* (Who made the first move? What did that person say or do?); and (3) *what happened then* (Who did and said what to whom? What were you thinking and feeling as the action went on? What ideas and emotions did your partner seem to have? How did it all come out?).

Here are some examples of the records we received:

Interaction No. 7, Husband's account
Setting: Afternoon golf game
Initiative: Betty, by making a mild comment about my golf game (which was in bad shape).
Sequence: Both of us were rather tired and hot. Betty had an equally bad day on the golf course. She commented on my game and I got mad and snapped back that she needn't pick on me considering my vulnerability as a poor golf player. This was too much for her (also the background variables) and she became livid, turned on her heel and marched off toward the car.

Interaction No. 7, Wife's account
Setting: Golf course, mid-afternoon
Initiative: Wife
Sequence: Neither of us were having a particularly good game and were irritated about that basically. Then, when Steve missed two putts, I said facetiously, "You're not concentrating." He got ticked off at the criticism and snapped back with something meaning mind your own business, which hurt my feelings, as I really had intended my comment lightly. A few minutes later someone (we were playing with a friend) mentioned being thirsty and Steve said there was a drinking fountain at the next hole. I pointed out that there was a hose right next to us and he replied with great ridicule about how much effort it would be to unscrew the hose, and so on, when there was a convenient fountain not far away. I despise being ridiculed and so I became incensed (the last straw, after the previous mind-your-own-business) and began to walk home (a 5 mile or so hike).

Here are some records from a couple in treatment.

Interaction No. 12, Husband's account
Setting: In automobile enroute to a family gathering
Initiative: Unless I did something I don't know about, Monica did
Sequence: The last few days had been going well including this particular morning until I asked her to sit next to me in the car to which she sarcastically replied, "I'm fine." This brought up all sorts of old feelings of resentment within me but rather than try and settle a dispute at a family function I decided to can it for another time. Later I smoked a couple cigarettes (which I'm not supposed to do according to an agreement but why adhere to an agreement like this when everything else is shitty between us). Upon discovering this she promptly walked up and put out the cigarette plus announcing that I was not to smoke in front of her. (This was in the presence of other people.) Again I did nothing. Then on the way home I was trying to take a nap (much German to do

when I got home). Had I been anyone else in the world she (Monica) would have afforded me the courtesy of keeping Susan [their daughter] from preventing my sleep. Twice I communicated (nonverbally) to her that I did not appreciate her actions (or lack of them). When it got to the point that she encouraged Susan to disturb me *I got Pissed!* I grabbed her by the hair and pulled her head my way a couple feet and informed her that I felt a little attitude rearrangement was in order.

One thing that really bothers me about this sequence of events is that she seemed to derive some pleasure or satisfaction out of aggravating me. I've never laid a hand on her forcibly before, but it became unbearable. She fails to take me seriously when I indicate I've about had it.

Interaction No. 12, Wife's account
Setting: In a car on the way to my brother's home — morning
Initiative: I guess I did
Sequence: David wanted me to sit next to him and I didn't feel like it then. I was comfortable where I was. David gave me his hurt angry look and nothing was really said all day. After we arrived at my brother's, he drank beer all day — quite a few. Then he started smoking my brother-in-law's cigarettes. We have an agreement that he only smoke cigarettes (not cigars or pipe) when I'm not around. It was obvious to me that he was doing it purposely although he tried to hide it a little. He was reaching for the lit cigarette from the ashtray when he saw me and then didn't pick it up. That happened twice. I finally picked it up from the ashtray and put it out in front of a couple of persons. David laughed and wondered what I was doing. He didn't smoke anymore but continued drinking. At one point when we were alone I asked him why he was smoking and he said, "Why not?" He then referred to the episode in the car. Nothing more was said.

We rode home with my parents. On the way home I didn't have a rejected feeling and acted as if nothing was wrong. I tried to get Dave to talk but he refused and attempted to sleep 3 hours home. First, though, because of my attitude he gave me a nasty hand sign, then called me some dirty names. Susan was sitting between us in the back seat and she'd climb on David and it made him mad 'cause I didn't stop her. He then pinched me on the leg hard. Susan continued and he kicked me two separate times. Susan tickled him and he pulled my hair, at which time I yelled, "Ouch!" Through the others I continued my attitude until the hairpulling. He told me to knock it off (he said I put Susan up to tickling him) and I yelled back to him to knock it off. My dad said, "What's going on back there?" David said, "We're having a few problems." After a few minutes my attitude was pleasant again. Since David kept pushing Susan away, I told her to stay in front when she wanted in back because Daddy didn't want her back there. He got mad about that.

By now we have obtained hundreds of records like these, from happy couples, not so happy couples, couples in therapy, couples who did not expect ever to need therapy. The interactions cover an enormously wide range of experience, bad times and good times, conflicts and conciliations, misunderstandings and the most intimate kinds of communion. I have yet to show anyone a set of records and not hear some remark about the sense of authenticity the accounts convey. Getting accurate accounts of important life experience is a difficult matter in psychology. Around-the-clock, direct observation can be conceived in fantasy, but in practical reality comprehensive observations are virtually impossible to conduct. Even sampled observations may be seriously reactive. When people know they are being observed, their behavior may change. Besides, the most subtle observations imaginable do not provide any information about subjective experiences. From my view, covert events are at least as interesting as explicit actions, and I will present some data shortly to show that internal events can be inferred in a decently reliable way from records such as these. Interaction records are not free of reactivity. There is every reason to suppose that people who expect to write accounts of their behavior will be affected by that expectation and will probably behave differently from the way they would if no reports were to be written. I see no way to eliminate indeterminacy from psychological inquiry. The best we can do is to gather information as unobtrusively as possible and then repeat the observations many times from multiple perspectives. If any identifiable signals come through the noise of several individually flawed measures, the regularities of complex social behavior may begin to grow clear.

The Interpretation of Interaction Records

Making sense out of free-response data is a difficult job. Any investigator who tries it is apt to wish the information had been collected in a more closely structured form. The goal of our research was not to confirm or disconfirm hypotheses, however, but to describe the natural processes of social interaction as faithfully as possible. At first we tried to fit various coding schemes developed by oiher investigators to the records before us. The Marital Interaction Coding System designed by Weiss, Hops, and Patterson (1973), the revised Leary code described by Terrill and Terrill (1965), and the coding system developed by Raush and his colleagues (1974) were all applied to samples of records. All of the codes fit, more or less, and allowed approximately the same levels of reliability the authors of the various schemes had previously reported. But none of the codes did justice to the material in the records, which seemed very rich in complex but apparently decipherable interpersonal meanings, and contained reports not only of the progressive actions of the participants but of their thoughts and feelings as well. I will not burden you with a tale of our labors to derive an alternative coding system. That is where the two years of "analysis" went, and many a preliminary code was discarded before a reasonably satisfactory one took form.

The procedure we finally used begins by segmenting each sequence into the main acts that make up the sequence, and goes on to the inference of an interpersonal meaning, or message, for each act. A brief record will illustrate the process.

Husband's Account
Setting: Kitchen, before dinner
Initiative: Beth
Sequence: Beth asked me to move a piece of bacon up so that she could put another piece in. I didn't know which way was up. Beth called me an ignoramus and said that north meant up and that I should have known that. I said that north didn't mean up to me. End of conversation.

Wife's Account
Setting: In the kitchen getting dinner ready
Initiative: (who started it?) I did
Sequence: I was trying to fix bacon and eggs for dinner and was trying to have everything ready at the same time. I asked Frank to help me put some bacon in the pan by moving the bacon up and making more room for the new pieces. He didn't know what to do and wound up slowing me down instead of helping. I got irritated and called him an ignoramus and wound up doing the job myself. Then we had dinner.

In the *Interaction Summary* for this sequence, several acts and messages were identified (see Figure 1).

Some arbitrariness is obviously involved in deciding how long and complex each "major" act is to be. Even greater arbitrariness appears to be involved in attributing meaning to the acts. Indeed, the primary rule for marking off acts is to designate a separate act whenever a new message appears in the sequence. Some strict behaviorists have expressed concern about the inferential leap our attributions of meaning require, and have correctly pointed out that any act might express interpersonal messages of many different kinds. A few psychoanalysts, on the other side, have said we do not go far enough with our interpretations and have suggested more elaborate psychodynamic constructions. The level of inference required to characterize our "mes-

Figure 1. Interaction Summary

Husband (H)	Wife (W)	Action	Message
	1	Asks H to move bacon "up"	Help me.
2		Asks W what "up" means.	I don't understand what you want me to do.
	3	Says "up" means "north"; calls H an ignoramus	You are stupid and incompetent
4		Says "up" doesn't mean "north" to him.	Your instructions were unclear. I had good cause for my confusion.
	5	Finishes preparing dinner.	I'll finish the job myself.

sages" seems to be about the same as that required to decode relational metacommunications as the Palo Alto communication analysts do (Jackson, Riskin, and Satir, 1961; Watzlawick, Beavin, and Jackson, 1967), or to interpret psychological meanings (as against social meanings) in transactional analysis (Berne, 1964; Harris, 1967). We could go deeper but doubt we could do so reliably. We might stay closer to the literal data but do not need to restrict our constructions on grounds of scientific rigor. The test of scientific acceptability for inferences such as these is not whether different interpretations are possible, but whether in fact different inferences are made by different judges.

To examine that question, five interaction records were presented to four advanced graduate students in clinical psychology. The action columns had already been completed in the records students received. The messages associated with these actions, according to the interpretations made earlier by the author and his associate, were randomly scrambled and presented to the students on a separate list. The students' task was to match the messages with the actions. Over all decisions, student judgments agreed with those of the primary investigators 87 percent of the time.

With the reliable inference of an interpersonal meaning for each act, the interpretation of records has gone a considerable way from unconstrained verbal account, but messages themselves contain further meanings. As our analyses eventually showed, the messages themselves are finite in form and content. Of all the things husbands and wives might say to each other in the course of their encounters, they do say only three kinds of things. First, they report some kind of *affect*.

Explicitly or implicitly, verbally or gesturally, every act a person performs in the presence of another expresses something about the emotional state the person is in at the time. Second, the messages report a *construal*. As these people reported their interactions, they were constantly interpreting their own behavior and that of their partners, making sense through those constructions of the interpersonal process in which they were taking part. Finally, every message asserts or implies an *expectation* regarding the subsequent behavior of the other. This is the "command" aspect of social communication as Bateson (1956) has defined it, though "command" seems too strong a term for the routine statements in most social messages. Always, as one person interacts with another, some expectation about the behavior of the other is expressed. Sometimes the expectation is of direct behavioral compliance. Sometimes the expectation is more subtle, for a twinge of guilt, a slight rise of sexual interest, or whatever other response one person might expect of the other.

The Main Forms of Affect, Construal, and Expectation Among Disturbed, Average, and Satisfied Married Couples

At least two sets of interaction records have been gathered so far for nineteen "satisfied" married couples who said they were happily married and denied having ever sought professional help for marital problems, thirty "average" couples who were not especially selected for marital satisfaction, and fourteen "disturbed" couples in treatment for marital difficulties. This sample of records was used to develop an inductive list of the affects, construals, and expectations the couples reported over all the acts in all the interactions the records described. At times independently and at other times cooperatively, the author and his research associate interpreted the acts one by one. For each act we wrote down the dominant affect, construal, and expectation the participant appeared to be displaying at the time. Over the 633 acts examined, eighteen different affective states were recorded more than once. These clustered into four main groups. First were some positive emotions, such as active affection, received affection (a sense of being loved), sexual arousal, and unspecified pleasure. Collectively, they formed an *Affection-Affiliation* cluster. Next were two distinct sets of negative feelings, *Aggression-Disapproval* (active regression, received injury, and so on) and *Distress-Dysphoria* (apprehension, depression, guilt, and the like). Finally, some acts were performed with relatively neutral affect, such as task attention, relief, or resignation. These represented a *Calm-Neutrality* cluster.

Twenty-two distinct construals appeared more than once over the full sample of acts, and again they seemed to fall into four main clusters. Some involved conceptions of a *Positive Relationship* (approval of other, approval of self, intimacy, empathy, trust, and such). Another large set suggested the perception of a *Negative Relationship* (disapproval of self or other, distance, distrust, and so on). The remaining two clusters of construal were also bipolar in apparent meaning. One set had to do with a *Sense of Control* (self responsible, autonomy, manageable situation) and the other with a *Loss of Control* (other responsible, domination, difficult situation).

Four general clusters of reciprocal response expectations also appeared, out of seventeen more specific expectations. In one set, people expected *Compliance* from their partners (compliance, concurrence, disclosure, acknowledgment of responsibility). In two other sets, various forms of *Positive Affect* and *Negative Affect* were anticipated. In a final cluster, all the actor wanted was for his or her partner to go away or reduce a demand. We called it *Withdrawal*.

As shown in Table 1, the three samples of married couples in our study differed widely in the frequencies with which major affects, construals, and expectations were registered. Clearly significant differences appeared for Affection, Aggression, and Distress, but not for Neutral Affect. Among construals, the groups differed in regard to perceptions of Positive and Negative Relationships, but not in Sense of Control or Loss of Control. All of the response expectation clusters,

Table 1. Frequencies of Major Classes of Affect, Construal, and Expectation for Disturbed, Average, and Satisfied Couples

	Disturbed Couples	Average Couples	Satisfied Couples	Total Sample
Affect				
Affection-Affiliation*	24 (.17)**	92 (.35)	97 (.43)	213
Calm-Neutrality	25 (.18)	56 (.21)	49 (.22)	130
Aggression-Disapproval*	61 (.43)	51 (.19)	59 (.26)	171
Distress-Dysphoria*	32 (.22)	65 (.25)	22 (.10)	119
Construal				
Positive Relationship	23 (.16)	101 (.38)	79 (.35)	203
Sense of Control	23 (.16)	56 (.21)	59 (.26)	138
Negative Relationship*	75 (.53)	67 (.26)	53 (.23)	195
Loss of Control	21 (.15)	40 (.15)	36 (.16)	97
Expectation				
Compliance*	43 (.30)	138 (.52)	92 (.40)	272
Positive Affect*	29 (.20)	61 (.23)	75 (.33)	165
Withdrawal*	42 (.30)	41 (.16)	49 (.22)	132
Negative Affect*	28 (.20)	24 (.09)	12 (.05)	64
Total Number of Acts	142	264	227	633

*X^2 significant at or beyond the .05 level.
**To reflect differences in sample size, proportional frequencies are shown in parentheses throughout the table.

Compliance, Positive Affect, Negative Affect, and Withdrawal, showed significant frequency differences across the groups.

Studies of Reliability

When such subtle processes as interpersonal communication and affective experience are examined, studies of reliability are even more urgently required than usual. The need is vividly illustrated by research on double-bind communications. According to the original double-bind hypothesis, as formulated by Bateson, Jackson and others in the Palo Alto Mental Research Institute (Bateson and others, 1956), parents of schizophrenics are especially disposed to the use of incongruent messages in communicating with their children. At one level, they say one thing. At another level they say something different and contradictory. The children are confused and in the extreme literally driven crazy by the garbled messages with which their parents keep bombarding them.

The double-bind idea is intriguing, and it has led to a mountainous body of research and further theory (Schuham, 1967). Not until the work had been going on for ten years, however, did anyone think to ask whether double-bind communications could be reliably identified or not. Ringuette and Kennedy (1966) gathered a set of letters the mothers of schizophrenic and nonschizophrenic patients had sent to their offspring and submitted these to some of the authors of the double-bind hypothesis. Each judge was asked to rate independently the degree to which the letters carried double-bind messages. The experts agreed with each other no better than chance.

Inferences required for the interpretation of interaction records can be made a good deal more reliably than that. Besides the study matching sequential acts with interpersonal meanings mentioned above, several other efforts have been made to see how closely judges agree in their perceptions of affect, construal, and expectation as reported in the records. Five records were presented to the same four students who did the matching study. A coding system for the classification of affects, construals, and expectations had previously been derived from the specific occurrences and major clusters described above. Judges were asked to code all records in the terms of this system, and their inferences were compared with those of the author and his wife, who had made the original interpretations from which the coding system was developed. Over all specific codes (eighteen affective states, twenty-two construals, and seventeen expectations), students' judgments agreed with those of the primary investigators in 69 percent of the cases. For the more general clusters of affect, construal, and expectation, the agreement value was 84 percent.

An attempt was then made to train the judges by discussing the classifications they had made, comparing them with those of the primary investigators, and clarifying both the definitions of the various categories and the decision rules by which the coding was done. Another set of records was submitted to the judges and agreement values computed as before. Reliabilities did not rise as we all had hoped. In fact, the percentages of agreement dropped slightly, to 68 percent and 77 percent for specific and general categories respectively. It is not clear why that happened. Probably the second five records, just by the chance of selection, were inherently more difficult to interpret than the first set. The interactions seemed more complex and the reports less clear. But even in the second set, agreement levels were higher than many people would expect. Over all judgments, agreement values come to 68 percent for specific codes and 79 percent for the general codes. *Kappa,* a statistic with many of the properties of a correlation coefficient but designed especially for use with categorical data (Cohen, 1960), yielded values of .67 and .71 for specific and general codes respectively. Considering the subjective quality of the processes under study, these levels of reliability are encouraging, though obviously it would be desirable to improve them.

One of the people in our group (Robinson, 1978) tried to improve reliability by interviewing married couples about their records. By talking with the participants, he hoped to fill in gaps in the records and to resolve disparities between the accounts of husbands and wives. Reliabilities improved a little, but not significantly. I hope I am wrong, but I now believe that the limits of attainable reliability for data such as these have been approached by the values stated above.

Analyses of Interaction Process

The conditions for a useful methodology of interpersonal relationships proposed early in this chapter require examination of process over time. The records themselves recount sequential events, but the flow of action and meaning, feeling and belief, expectation and response in any interaction is exceedingly complex. The interaction sequences in our sample ranged in length from two to fourteen acts. For each act, any of eighteen affects, twenty-two construals, and seventeen expectations might occur. For an average sequence of five acts, the number of possible combinations of affects, construals, and expectations is 6732^{10}. Even if the process is simplified by considering only general clusters of feeling, belief, and expectation, over eleven sextellion combinations are possible. Some progress has been made by Raush and others (1974) and Gottman, Markman, and Notarious (1977) in developing systematic approaches to the analysis of interaction sequences. The work done so far, however, has been limited to chains of unidimensional reciprocal acts. The first act is assigned a single code, the response of the partner also receives a single code, and so forth throughout the sequence. The statistical procedures necessary to accommodate sequential data of varying lengths and for which each element in any sequence displays multiple characteristics simultaneously have not yet appeared, though there is no reason they cannot be developed in principle. Until more refined procedures come along, simpler analyses will have to do.

The process studies we have done so far have been limited to *interaction cycles,* that is, the action-reaction couplets that make up any sequence. For any cycle the first act may be called a *statement* and the second a *reply.* Within any sequence of more than two acts, each reply also becomes a statement preceding the following reply of the partner. Each cycle interlocks with the one before it, like the links of a chain, until the sequence ends. The number of interaction cycles in any sequence is one less than the number of acts in the sequence.

Even interaction cycles are complex, but of all the combinations of affect, construal, and expectation that might occur in the exchanges of husbands and wives, only a small number actually occur often enough to be of much interest. Frequencies were tabulated over the 507 interaction cycles in the entire samples of records. The most common cycle was one of mutual enjoyment. The interpersonal statement is an invitation. "Let's have a good time together." "Yes, let's," says the partner. For both people, feelings of pleasure, perceptions of intimacy in an enjoyable setting, and expectations of cooperative behavior follow. The second most common cycle begins with an appeal for support. The initiator feels distressed (apprehension, depression, fatigue), regards the situation as unmanageable, sees himself or herself as inadequate and often as misunderstood by the partner, and asks for affection and help from the other.

Interpersonal statement: "I'm down; I need your support."
Interpersonal reply: "Of course, I'm on your side."

Two kinds of conflict patterns appeared. Both start with the same message ("I hate you, dislike you, disapprove of you"), both involve feelings of active aggression, a construal that the other is responsible for whatever has given rise to the anger, and an expectation that the other will feel some pain and acknowledge responsibility for the state the angry one is in. Two different reactions may follow, however. In one pattern, most common among couples in clinical treatment, the person under attack whines off in injured withdrawal. "I feel hurt and misunderstood; I'm withdrawing from you and want you to get away from me." In another conflict pattern, the person under attack retaliates: "The hell it's my fault; you are responsible too." Instead of received injury, active aggression appears as the dominant affect. In our sample of disturbed couples, this Aggression-Retaliation cycle was never reported. Fighting it out in this assertive way was most commonly seen among the satisfied couples.

Two common cycles have to do with behavior in task situations. In one set, the partners cooperate. In the other they do not. The main difference between the two cycles is in the way the initiating statement is made. When cooperation occurs, the request usually involves an assumption of mutual responsibility and shared effort. "Let's get this job of ours done." Refusals to cooperate were usually brought on by "dumping." One partner assumed the other should do all or most of the work: "Let's you get going." The "dumpee" disagreed, with feeling.

A fairly common cycle is made up of affectionate strokes. "I love you," says one. "I love you too," says the other. Another comes after quarrels, and shows how people get back together again. The most interesting feature of the conciliation pattern is that it involves construals of empathy and personal responsibility. People in our study patched up their quarrels most successfully when they attended to the other's views and took initiatory responsibility for repairing whatever damage had been done.

Besides the conflict patterns mentioned above, the three groups of couples differed in the frequencies with which several other cycles were registered. In these reports of the most significant interaction for a day, not a single cycle of mutual enjoyment was reported by the couples in treatment, though enjoyable exchanges were reported nineteen times by "satisfied" couples and thirteen times by those in the "average" sample. Only once did a disturbed couple report mutual affection, though eleven such cycles appeared in the records of satisfied couples. Other differences appeared as well. I do not want to make too much of them because the numbers of cases are small and the findings have not been cross-validated. The patterns that have emerged so far, however, seem interesting both clinically and scientifically, and I hope to see them investigated more closely in the future.

Where Next

Now that some common interactions of married life have been described, it would seem reasonable to direct extended but more finely grained inquiries to some of the more interesting patterns that the first exploration revealed. The decision to ask for records of "significant" interactions in our reconaissance was more or less arbitrary. If an investigator should choose to focus more strictly on conflict patterns, or affectional ones, or sexual ones, or exchanges of any more specific kind, more detailed information about those kinds of interactions should not be difficult to obtain.

Different ways of analyzing the data should also be explored. There is nothing coercive about the coding system we developed. In fact it would be highly desirable to see if the most important information in our scheme cannot be expressed more simply. The system we used allows the derivation of secondary indices of several kinds. "Adequacy of communication" scores, for instance, could be calculated by counting the number of times the construals of one partner correspond with the just prior messages (and implicit construals) of the other. "Effectiveness of influence" might be a more powerful concept than "dominance," and effectiveness of influence might be defined by counting the number of times the assertive expectations of one partner are followed by compliant responses on the part of the other. The general affective tone of a relationship might be gauged by aggregating affective occurrences over sets of interactions. "Satisfaction-dissatisfaction" scores might be obtained, for example, by comparing discrepancies in the frequency of Distress-Dysphoria and Aggression-Disapproval with those of Affection-Affiliation. Degrees of "Emotional turbulence" might be measured by the collective preponderance of the three clusters just named relative to the frequency of "Calm-Neutrality." Once the flow of affective, cognitive, and behavioral events has been described over a set of interactions, the more general characteristics of the relationship should not be difficult to derive.

Of course it is essential to go beyond interaction records in any comprehensive effort to study interpersonal process in natural settings. Records offer some advantages over other means of obtaining information about social behavior. Unlike most questionnaires they deal with active processes rather than static traits. Unlike most interviews they register events immediately after they have happened and are therefore more likely to provide accurate, detailed accounts of the events. But interaction records are still self-reports and need to be examined in reference to other kinds of data. Naturalistic observation of interaction process is extremely difficult. Besides the problem of reactivity mentioned earlier in this chapter, serious ethical and practical constraints inhibit any effort to gather representative samples of significant interactions in the daily lives of human beings. People will not usually allow psychologists to invade their bedrooms or kitchens; and, even if they do, many of the most important events may happen somewhere else, on the golf course or in a car on the way to visit relatives. Still, we psychologists must do better than we have with direct observation if we are serious about building a natural science of social behavior. The work of Patterson, Weiss and others of the Oregon research group (Weiss, Hops, and Patterson, 1973) offers some encouragement along these lines. Some recent innovations by Christensen (1978) also seem very promising. Christensen placed omnidirectional microphones connected to a cassette recorder at strategic locations in the homes of couples with whom he was working clinically, programmed activation of the recorders randomly, and obtained some exceedingly interesting samples of live interactions between the husbands and wives he was trying to help. Of course we must continue to contrive situations deliberately to elicit interaction patterns of particular interest, to create experimental analogs of the natural processes we are trying to understand. Various forms of interpersonal process recall (Kagan, 1973), in which video-taped interactions are replayed to participants and their reactions to the display are recorded, seem to offer particularly rich information about the covert processes as well as the observable expressions of interpersonal behavior.

Then data from all the sources must be coordinated. When we first proposed multimodal studies of interpersonal relationships, I simplemindedly presumed that the main problems in coordinating data across modes would be correlational, that is, that some kind of process-sensitive multitrait-multimethod analysis would solve most of our problems. I still regard issues of convergent and discriminant validity as very important ones, though the issues are rarely appreciated by investigators in social psychology. Olson and Rabunsky (1972) found four measures of "family power" to be negligibly correlated, though the authors who had employed each of the measures in previous studies wrote as if they were examining power relationships generally. Bernal and her colleagues (1976) compared observations of child behavior at home with observations in school and found the highest home-to-school correlation among the various indexes employed to be negative, but not statistically significant. Martin and others (1976) studied parent-child interactions in two different analog situations and in the home. Behavior in one analog was essentially unrelated to behavior in the other, and the highest correlations among behavioral indexes in the laboratory situations and in the home were some negative correlations for fathers. As clearly as Mischel (1968) and others of us have shown the impact of situational influence on behavior, many people still do not seem to realize that data-collecting operations are situations too, and that the representations of behavior that appear in clinical accounts and research protocols are bound to vary from one method to another. If we want to find out which of any consistencies that appear are a function of behavior rather than method, there is no way to proceed but to examine the same behavioral events by multiple means and to determine convergences across operations.

As I go ahead with the multimodal assessment of interaction process, however, I am coming to suspect that many of the problems in coordinating data are too complex to be examined with simple convergence designs. The kinds of data obtained from interviews, observations, records, and analogs, for example, often seem qualitatively different, and efforts to compare them quantitatively through any simple correlational analysis may be misguided. Instead, the most appropriate aim may be to specify what kinds of operations are most useful for obtaining which kinds of information and then to integrate data from various sources into coherent statements about the phenomena we are trying to describe. The need to tailor methods to the particular processes under study has become most noticeable to me as other relationships besides marriage are examined. One of our students at Rutgers is trying to figure out what goes on in the "healing" works of Cuban-American *Santeros*, for example. Many Cuban immigrants go to spiritualists for help with physical and emotional problems. In the interactions between *Santeros* and supplicants, various rituals are performed. Supernatural forces are invoked. In successful cases, spiritual possession is literally thought to occur at some stage in the process, and later the spirits must be properly exorcised. The patterns of affect, construal, and expectation that go on in these sessions should be mighty interesting, but we do not expect interaction records of the kind we found useful with married couples to be appropriate. Some of the participants are illiterate, for one thing. Other methods will be needed, and some of them will probably have to be designed uniquely for the project. Other people here at Rutgers are interested in interaction patterns between therapists and clients, parents and children, and gay lovers, to name only a few of the relationships we are trying to explore. The general concept of relationship as a pattern of recurrent interaction sequences seems to be holding up quite well. Study of the interpersonal messages, and then the emotions, beliefs, and reciprocal demands that go on through the sequences has also kept its value, though the particular forms of affect, construal, and expectation that matter most in one relationship may never even occur in another. New variants of method and new coding systems for the interpretation of data seem to be required for each relationship. When several different relationships have been examined, some of the affective, cognitive, and behavioral characteristics may show up in them all. It will be interesting to see what those common processes look like. Right now I would be hesitant to guess.

In the more distant future, the concept of interaction process should be extended. So far, all we can describe clearly is an individual interaction sequence. If relationships are defined by reference to recurrent interaction patterns, better ways must be developed for determining when two interactions belong together as members of the same pattern and when they are different enough to form separate patterns. The linkages between earlier and later interactions have to be examined if the developmental courses of relationships are to be understood. The conditions that maintain stability in relationships, and those that transform relationships, are vitally important to clinicians and should be of interest to social psychologists as well. Sound professional practice can only be based on dependable natural science. I sometimes get discouraged about the study of interpersonal relationships. The complexities of interaction process seem to reach no limit, and progress toward resolution of those complexities seems glacially slow. Most of the time, though, I have been able to persuade myself that the concepts and methods we need are beginning to take shape.

References

Bateson, G., and others. "Toward a Theory of Schizophrenia." *Behavioral Science,* 1956, *1,* 251–264.

Bernal, M. E., and others. "Comparison of Boys' Behavior in Homes and Classrooms." In E. J. Mash, L. A. Hamerlynck, and L. C. Handy (Eds.), *Behavior Modification and Families.* New York: Brunner/Mazel, 1976.

Berne, E. *Games People Play.* New York: Grove Press, 1964.

Campbell, D. T., and Fiske, D. W. "Convergent and Discriminant Validation by the Multitrait-Multimethod Matrix." *Psychological Bulletin,* 1959, *56,* 81–105.

Carson, R. C. *Interaction Concepts of Personality.* Chicago: Aldine, 1969.

Christensen, A. *Naturalistic Observation of Families: A System for Random Audio Recordings in the Home.* Department of Psychology, University of California at Los Angeles, 1978.

Cohen, J. "A Coefficient for Agreement of Nominal Scales." *Educational and Psychological Measurement,* 1960, *20.* 37–46.

Endler, N. S., and Hunt, J. M. "Sources of Behavioral Variance as Measured by the S-R Inventory of Anxiousness." *Psychological Bulletin,* 1966, *65,* 336–346.

Gottman, J., Markman, H., and Notarious, C. "A Typography of Marital Conflict: A Sequential Analysis of Verbal and Nonverbal Behavior." *Journal of Marriage and the Family,* 1977, *39,* 461–477.

Harris, T. A. *I'm OK — You're OK: A Practical Guide to Transactional Analysis.* New York: Harper and Row, 1967.

Homans, G. C. *Social Behavior: Its Elementary Forms.* New York: Harcourt, Brace, and World, 1961.

Jackson, D. D., Riskin, J., and Satir, V. "A Method of Analysis of a Family Interview." *Archives of General Psychiatry,* 1961, *5,* 321–386.

Kagan, N. "Can Technology Help Us toward Reliability in Influencing Human Interaction?" *Educational Technology,* 1973, *13,* 44–51.

Martin, S., and others. "The Comparability of Behavioral Data in Laboratory and Natural Settings." In E. J. Mash, L. A. Hamerlynck, and L. C. Handy (Eds.), *Behavior Modification and Families.* New York: Brunner/Mazel, 1976.

Mischel, W. *Personality and Assessment.* New York: Wiley, 1968.

Olson, D. H., and Rabunsky, C. "Validity of Four Measures of Family Power." *Journal of Marriage and the Family,* 1972, *34,* 224–234.

Peterson, D. R. *The Clinical Study of Social Behavior.* New York: Appleton-Century-Crofts, 1968.

Peterson, D. R. "A Functional Approach to the Study of Person-Person Interactions." In D. Magnusson and N. S. Endler (Eds.), *Personality at the Crossroads: Current Issues in Interactional Psychology.* Hillsdale, N.J.: Erlbaum, 1977.

Peterson, D. R. *Assessing Interpersonal Relationships by Means of Interaction Records.* New Brunswick, N.J.: Graduate School of Applied and Professional Psychology, Rutgers University, 1978.

54

Raush, H. L., and others. *Communication, Conflict, and Marriage.* San Francisco: Jossey-Bass, 1974.

Ringuette, E. L., and Kennedy, T. "An Experimental Study of the Double-Bind Hypothesis." *Journal of Abnormal Psychology,* 1966, *71,* 136–141.

Robinson, D. L. "The Reliability of Written Reports and Verbal Inquiry in Assessing Marital Interactions." Unpublished master's thesis, Rutgers University, 1978.

Schuham, A. I. "The Double-Bind Hypothesis a Decade Later." *Psychological Bulletin,* 1967, *68,* 409–416.

Sells, S. B. *Stimulus Determinants of Behavior.* New York: Ronald Press, 1963.

Strodtbeck, F. T. "Husband-Wife Interaction over Revealed Differences." *American Sociological Review,* 1951, *16,* 468–473.

Terrill, J., and Terrill, R. "A Method for Studying Family Communication." *Family Process,* 1965, *4,* 259–290.

Thibaut, J. W., and Kelley, H. H. *The Social Psychology of Groups.* New York· Wiley, 1959.

Watzlawick, P., Beavin, J. H., and Jackson, D. D. *Pragmatics of Human Communication.* New York: Norton, 1967.

Weiss, R. L., Hops, H., and Patterson, G. R. "A Framework for Conceptualizing Marital Conflict: A Technology for Altering It, Some Data for Evaluating It." In L. A. Hamerlynck, L. C. Handy, and E. J. Mash (Eds.), *Behavior Change: Methodology, Concepts, and Practice.* Champaign, Ill.: Research Press, 1973.

Donald R. Peterson is professor of psychology and dean of the Graduate School of Applied and Professional Psychology at Rutgers, the State University of New Jersey.

Described and evaluated in this chapter is a general theory and method of person-situation interaction, which emphasizes the interrelationship between the person and the environment — and the complex processes which underlie that relationship — by focusing on the goodness-of-fit between characteristics of the person and properties of the environment(s) to which he or she is commonly exposed.

Interaction as Person-Environment Fit

Richard A. Kulka

Person-situation interactions are often conceptualized in diffuse or unspecified ways, and the precise nature of either the elements or the process implied is rarely given adequate attention. In part, of course, this ambiguity reflects confusion in terminology, since the concept of "interaction" has been subject to widely varied and often vague uses. According to Olweus (1977), for example, at least four different meanings of the term *interaction* are used in the literature: (1) combination or connection; (2) interdependency; (3) reciprocal action; and (4) statistical interaction; and each meaning implies a somewhat different logical and methodological approach to the study of person-situation interaction. Even this attempt at clarification is, however, somewhat illusory: for example, statistical interaction or non-additivity in itself may take an almost infinite variety of forms (Southwood, 1978).

One form of statistical interaction is suggested by models of person-environment congruence or fit, which have now emerged in virtually every major domain of social research (Feather, 1975; French,

Preparation of this chapter was supported in part by research grants from the National Institute of Education (G-78-0049) and the National Institute of Mental Health (MH-26006). The author expresses his great appreciation to John R. P. French, Jr., for his helpful suggestions in preparing this chapter, and to Lynn R. Kahle for his skillful editing of earlier drafts of the manuscript.

Rodgers, and Cobb, 1974; Getzels, 1969; Holland, 1973; Kahana, 1978; Kulka, Mann, and Klingel, 1978; Lawler, 1973; Locke, 1969; Moos, 1974; Pervin, 1968; Stern, 1970; Veroff and Feld, 1970). The concept of person-environment [P-E] congruence focuses on the extent to which characteristics of the person match those of the environment to which he or she is commonly exposed, assuming that the better the fit the more favorable the consequences for the person (Feather, 1972; Pervin, 1968).

A Model of Person-Environment Fit

Although several of the models cited above could be used to describe and illustrate the implications of conceptualizing person-situation interaction as congruence or fit, one particular model, that developed by French, Rodgers, and Cobb (1974), seems particularly suitable for that task because it appears both flexible enough to incorporate essential features of the others and yet sufficiently comprehensive to account for a variety of research findings. The basic assumption of the model, which has now been elaborated in a number of papers (Caplan and others, 1975; French, Rodgers, and Cobb, 1974; Harrison, 1976, 1978; Kulka, 1976), is that adjustment may be conceived of as the goodness-of-fit between characteristics of the person and properties of his or her environment.

Basic Concepts. The theory may be described in terms of a few basic concepts. First, the model proposes four basic elements: (1) the *objective environment,* which includes aspects of the physical and social world that exist independently of the person's perceptions of them; (2) the *subjective environment,* representing the person's perceptions and cognitions of relevant aspects of his or her objective environment; (3) the *objective person,* referring to the objectively demonstrable characteristics of the person (such as needs, values, abilities, and other attributes which are relatively enduring), independent of his or her perceptions; and (4) the *subjective person,* the individual's reported perceptions or cognitions of his or her characteristics (the self-concept or self-identity of the person). Employing these four elements, the model distinguishes between *subjective* person-environment fit, where both characteristics of the person and the environment are assessed as perceived and reported by the person, and *objective* person-environment fit, where both components are measured independent of the person's perceptions and cognitions of them.

Second, the theory proposes that for both objective and subjective P-E fit there are two basic subtypes, describable in terms of two sorts of demands and two corresponding forms of supplies to meet these demands. The motives (needs or values) of the *person* represent one type of demand, which may or may not be met by *environmental* supplies in the form of opportunities for gratification. The other form of demand emanates from the environment in terms of role demands or requirements, where the supplies to meet such demands consist of the skills or abilities of the person. The model assumes that both forms of misfit are indicators of poor adjustment and will be related to various forms of psychological (low self-esteem, job dissatisfaction, depression) or physiological strain (any deviation from normal responses in the person), as well as to various coping or reactive behaviors.

Predicted Relationships Between P-E Fit and Strain. Hypothesized relationships between various dimensions of P-E fit and strains are generally represented by one of three hypothetical functions, as illustrated in Figure 1. Curve A illustrates a monotonic curvilinear relationship between size of deficiency for a particular resource or ability and a given measure of strain, with excess of either environmental or personal supplies having no influence on level of strain. Thus, the curve of strain plotted against P-E fit decreases as the magnitude of

Figure 1. Three Hypothetical Person-Environment Fit Curves

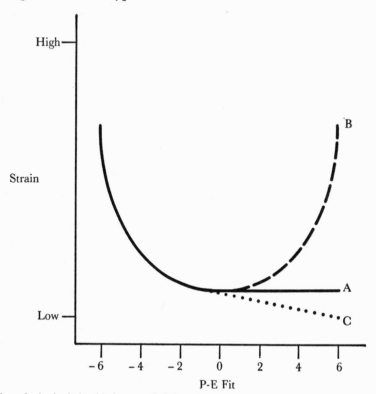

The hypothesized relationship between P-E fit and psychological strain as adapted from French, Rodgers, and Cobb (1974).

deficiency decreases, reaching an asymptote at perfect fit and showing no further changes with increasing excesses of supplies. For example, a thirsty man will drink until he has quenched his thirst, beyond which additional supplies of water would not result in greater satisfaction.

In contrast, the other two curves reflect hypotheses which suggest that excess supplies or abilities will make a difference. In one instance (Curve B) the relationship between fit and strain is U-shaped, strain being lowest at the point of perfect fit, but rising with increases in *either* deficiency *or* excess. This type of relationship is proposed where two or more important motives are involved and the presence of excess supplies for one motive may result in deficient supplies for another. For example, if academic abilities are exceeded by teacher demands, strain would result as in the left half of Curve A; however, as abilities increasingly exceed demands, boredom, apathy, or resentment may result as a consequence of the frustration or lack of opportunity to use a valued skill.

A similar example illustrates the hypothesis suggested by Curve C, whereby excess supplies may result in *decreased* levels of strain. Such relationships are posited when excess supplies for one motive can be used directly as (or exchanged for) supplies for other motives. Accordingly, students whose reading abilities exceed the level of difficulty of materials used for reading instruction may show fewer behavioral symptoms of strain than those whose ability matches the material because a variety of other rewards (for instance, teacher praise, grades) may be associated with that relationship (Jorgenson, 1977).

Empirical relationships approximating each of these hypothetical functions have been reported in many of the studies cited above. One good example is presented by Caplan and his colleagues (1975) in a study of workers in twenty-three occupations. In that study, a multiple item measure of job complexity P-E fit was derived by subtracting the amount of complexity preferred by the individual (subjective person) from the amount of complexity perceived on the job (subjective environment). The relationship between person-environment fit on job complexity and a clinically-validated index of depression approximated well the hypothetical U-shaped relationship illustrated in Figure 1. Depression was lowest for those with perfect fit and increased with either too little or too much job complexity (Harrison, 1978). Additional examples of several empirical relationships approximating each of the nonlinear forms predicted by the model are available from a recent study of P-E fit among students at two Detroit suburban high schools (Kulka, 1976; Kulka, Klingel, and Mann, 1978).

Conceptual and Methodological Issues

This summary should serve to illustrate the basic logic and utility of conceiving of person-situation interactions as congruence or fit.

Associated with implementing such perspectives, however, are a number of basic conceptual and methodological issues, most of which are shared with other research approaches to the study of person-situation interaction (Pervin, 1968). For example, should one consider the subjective or objective person and environment? Should the same units of analysis be employed for persons and environments? How should P-E fit scores be calculated? What are the alternative functional or quantitative relationships which best describe various types of P-E congruence? Since these questions are some of the most central facing researchers who wish to investigate P-E fit, important aspects of each will be examined here. These and a number of other significant issues are discussed at greater length by Kulka (1976) and Harrison (1976).

Subjective versus Objective Assessment of Person/Environment. While the basic dialectic between those concerned with objective characteristics of the environment and those who employ subjective or phenomenological approaches has a long history in psychology (Ekehammer, 1974), the distinction between subjective and objective person may be at least as significant for research on person-situation interaction as that between perceived and "actual" environment (French, Rodgers, and Cobb, 1974). Yet few studies of P-E congruence have employed even crude measures of the objective environment, and fewer still attempt to assess characteristics of the person independent of the individual's perceptions.

Although in some cases the choice of subjective measures has been deliberate (Feather, 1972; Locke, 1969), the predominant use of perceptions as indicators of, or to the exclusion of, objective measures is primarily a reflection of the pragmatic difficulties associated with developing good objective measures of P-E fit. The use of demographic characteristics of individuals as proxies for the objective characteristics of either person or environment (Veroff and Feld, 1970) provides only a crude (and non-commensurate) approximation of the constructs desired. Similarly, studies which employ a mean of "consensual" perceived environment rating as an indicator of objective environment rest on the dubious assumption that inhabitants of a common setting all experience the same environment (Moos, 1974; Schneider and Bartlett, 1970). Essentially, objective assessment procedures must recognize that each individual occupies a relatively unique set of sub-environments within a particular setting without lapsing completely to a phenomenological frame of reference. Based on this assumption, several researchers have proposed structured observations of environmental dimensions *at the individual level* (for instance, Jenkins and others, 1975).

The major problem with subjective measures is, of course, that perceptions of either the individual or the environment may be influenced or distorted by personal characteristics of the respondent. Nevertheless, such relationships are neither invariably found (Hall, 1970; Marks, 1968) nor inherently undesirable. In particular, to the extent that relationships between environmental perceptions and individual characteristics reflect the mediating role of sub-environments or of role positions (Moos, 1974), such subjective measures may often provide a more accurate approximation of the "actual" environment than many of the rather crude objective measures employed to date.

Overall, little research evidence clearly points to the superiority of either an objective or subjective methodology for the prediction of behavior. The issue is really less a question of "Which determines behavior?" than of "What are the differences in the determinative impact of each?" or "Under what circumstances is one or the other type of data more useful?" Since such circumstances are not yet well-established, the strategy of collecting both kinds of measures wherever possible is well-advised (Pervin, 1968). It may well be, for example, that differences in measurement on the objective-subjective continuum account for many of the inconsistencies apparent in the research literature on person-situation interactions.

Persons and Environments: Should the Same Units Be Used? Because the concept of fit specifically emphasizes the matching of individual to environmental variables, a number of theorists have argued that P-E fit can best be assessed only when persons and environments are described and measured in terms of logically related concepts and in commensurable units (Bem, this volume; French, Rodgers, and Cobb, 1974; Graham, 1976). In essence, while approaches to person-environment interaction that employ commensurate units are hardly applicable to all interactional phenomena, within their range of applicability they have at least two distinct advantages. First, persons and environments can be *quantitatively* compared only when the same dimensions are used for measuring each (French and Kahn, 1962; Lewin, 1951). Second, contingent on the concreteness of the actual dimensions employed, the use of commensurate measures may permit a clearer and more direct understanding of the sources and consequences of P-E interaction than that provided by non-commensurate approaches.

Non-commensurate dimensions, as Harrison (1976) notes, have been used to study P-E fit for at least three legitimate reasons: (1) interest in either individual or environmental characteristics at a sociological (demographic or ecological) level (Hackman and Lawler, 1971); (2) to continue research on non-commensurate measures that have a previously established empirical utility (Veroff and Feld, 1970); and (3) the need for economy in measurement and analysis. In each case, however, interactions are generally explained by assuming that they reflect processes occurring on commensurate dimensions of fit. Thus, although the current primitive state of psychological measurement has not yet permitted a fully convincing demonstration of the quantitative advantages of a commensurate approach, the description of person-environment relationships in precise quantitative terms is clearly our long-term aspiration, since only through the development of such quantitative models will it be possible to use logic and mathematics to attain consistent and non-contradictory theories for such phenomena (French and Kahn, 1962; Harris, 1976).

Measuring Person-Environment Fit. With very few exceptions, measures of P-E fit represent some variant (algebraic, absolute, cumulative, and so on) of a "raw difference" score, formed by subtracting a measure of environment from a commensurate measure of the person, or vice versa. In proposing the use of such two-part indices, however, investigators of congruence have not fully recognized important criticisms of the use of difference, "gain," or "change" scores in other research contexts (Bohrnstedt, 1969; Cronbach and Furby, 1970; Kessler, 1977). In general, most critics agree that raw differences have a number of undesirable limitations and can easily lead to fallacious conclusions.

Some of the potential pitfalls or liabilities associated with the use of discrepancy scores as indices of fit involve basic scaling problems, such as the assumption of commensurate *and* interval scaling (Cronbach, 1958; French, Rodgers, and Cobb, 1974; Lord, 1963), the "physicalism-subjectivism dilemma" (Bereiter, 1963; Imparato, 1972), and problems in assessing profile similarity (Cronbach and Gleser, 1953; Nunnally, 1962). Other limitations are more statistical in nature, including issues of unreliability, variance, "regression toward the mean," and a host of other potential artifacts associated with the fact that relationships involving difference scores can be expressed as exact mathematical functions of the intercorrelations, correlations, and variances of their components (Blau and Duncan, 1967; Bohrnstedt, 1969).

Despite these and a number of other potential hazards or pitfalls associated with the use of raw discrepancy scores, however, most alternative methods are also subject to important limitations. For example, equity theories (Lawler, 1973) suggest that P-E fit should be calculated as a ratio (E/P or P/E), but potential liabilities associated with the analyses of ratio variables are at least as numerous and complex as those involving difference scores (Chayes, 1971; Fuguitt and Lieberson, 1974; Schuessler, 1974). Second, the use of product-moment or rank-order correlation coefficients as measures of P-E fit (Feather, 1972; Pelz and Andrews, 1966) has at least two potential drawbacks: (1) since they are measures of covariation rather than of agreement (Robinson, 1957), individuals with rather large discrepancies between P and E may nevertheless have coefficients equal to unity because of identical relative scale magnitudes, whereas other respondents with P and E scores of comparable size may have zero or even negative correlations, due to small chance fluctuations in order (Feldman and Newcomb, 1969; Stern, 1970); and (2) the true meaning of low or zero correlations is somewhat ambiguous, since randomness of responding and poor P-E fit are completely confounded in such scores (Wylie, 1974). Third, while difference scores may be avoided entirely by having respondents make direct judgments of the magnitude of discrepancy between P and E, such measures may be more subject to cognitive or perceptual bias and distortion than two-part indices and, in any case, are conceptually appropriate only for subjective discrepancies (Wylie, 1974).

The ultimate way, of course, to avoid the limitations of difference scores in not to derive measures of P-E fit at all. Thus, Cronbach and Furby (1970) argue that the computation and use of differences between two values to define individual scores indicative of a construct should be abandoned in favor of multivariate approaches using the two variables separately in analysis so as to allow for complex relationships (Blau and Duncan, 1967). Nevertheless, it is also possible to argue, as Wylie (1974) does, that, since a P-E discrepancy is presumably something an individual can experience as a real difference, a valid theoretical reason exists for trying to operationalize it by a subtractive score, albeit as free as possible of irrelevant influences. This claim carries, of course, a considerable burden of proof, and, if results of future research from this perspective prove to be unconvincing, discrepancy score methods may indeed need to be abandoned for the measurement of P-E fit.

Functional or Quantitative Representations of P-E Fit Relationships. A major advantage of commensurate dimension approaches to the study of person-environment fit is that they not only allow one to determine whether various outcomes are related to P-E discrepancies, but they also permit the evaluation of various quantitative representations of the relationship between P-E fit and such criteria. These relationships may vary in a number of important ways (shape, directionality, the significance of perfect fit), and an appreciation of these alternatives is important precisely because such quantitative hypotheses influence the selection of methodology, which in turn influences the probability of obtaining interpretable results.

Congruence Along a Single Dimension. Models of P-E fit represent only a subset of possible models of P-E interaction, but the potential range of variation in congruence relationships is far greater than that implied by Figure 1. Essentially, the three shapes illustrated there are only a subset of the many theoretical functions which may be obtained by various combinations of at least five properties of relationships:

(1) continuous or noncontinuous, (2) monotonic or nonmonotonic, (3) one-directional or two-directional, (4) linear or nonlinear, and (5) symmetrical or asymmetrical. Using the first two properties in particular, we can distinguish, as Kahana (1978) does, three broad sets of functional models: cumulative difference, critical difference, and optimal congruence models. Cross-cutting these model types, additional differences relate to linearity, directionality and symmetry of congruence relationships. One-directional models, for example, hypothesize the existence of relationships between incongruence and outcomes on only one side of perfect fit. Two directional models propose such relationships for both positive and negative discrepancies. Moreover, while one-directional models are inherently asymmetrical, two directional models may be either symmetrical or asymmetrical. That is, the consequences of incongruence may differ depending on the direction (positive or negative) of the P-E fit difference.

Cumulative Difference models assume that the effects of incongruence are cumulative and continuous. They generally, though not always, suggest that the greater the P-E difference on a given dimension, the more negative the anticipated outcomes, with perfect fit or zero mismatch hypothesized to result in the most positive outcomes. As illustrated in Figure 2, cumulative difference models may be one- or two-directional, linear or nonlinear, and symmetrical or asymmetrical. Such cumulative difference models of P-E fit are by far the most commonly proposed, and empirical relationships approximating each of the functions illustrated in Figure 2 have been reported in the literature.

Critical Difference models (shown in Figure 3) consider the possibility that the effects of mismatch or lack of fit may be problematic, detrimental, or perhaps even positive (Feldman and Newcomb, 1969) only beyond a certain critical point or range. Thus, to determine the impact of incongruence, one must specify such critical parameters (point or range), which may either be absolute or vary according to the individual. In addition to possible differences in directionality and symmetry, such models may also be either *continuous,* where the point of critical difference serves as a starting point for a cumulative function, or *noncontinuous,* whereby the effect of mismatch is clearly distinguished at the critical point from the effects of congruence.

In contrast with cumulative and critical difference models, which generally assume that incongruence has negative consequences, while perfect fit results in positive outcomes, *optimal congruence* models suggest the possibility of a curvilinear or U-shaped relationship, whereby both perfect fit *and* extreme mismatch between individual and environment may have *positive* outcomes (Feldman and Newcomb, 1969; Hall, 1970). In addition to differences in directionality and symmetry, optimal congruence models, illustrated in Figure 4, may be distin-

Figure 2. Cumulative Difference Models of Person-Environment Fit
(Linear and Nonlinear)

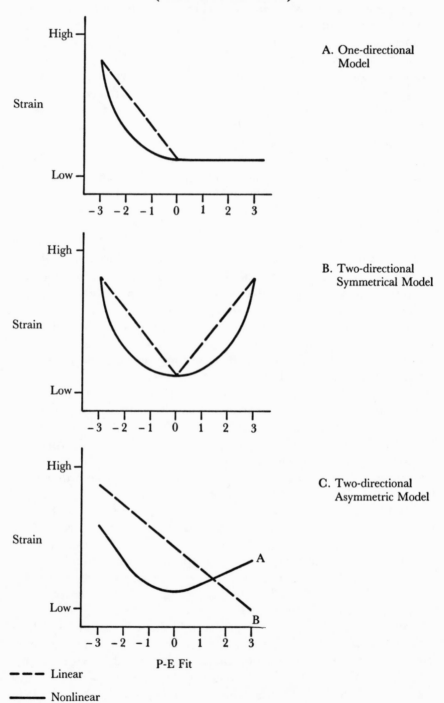

A. One-directional
   Model

B. Two-directional
   Symmetrical Model

C. Two-directional
   Asymmetric Model

- - - Linear

—— Nonlinear

Figure 3. Critical Difference Models of Person-Environment Fit
(Continuous and Non-Continuous)

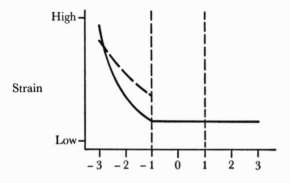

A. One-directional
Model

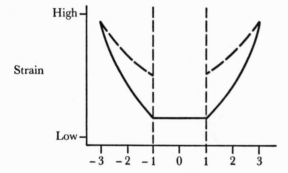

B. Two-directional
Symmetrical Model

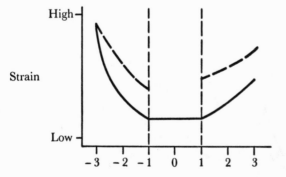

C. Two-directional
Asymmetric Model

——— Continuous

- - - Non-Continuous

Figure 4. Optimal Congruence Models of Person-Environment Fit

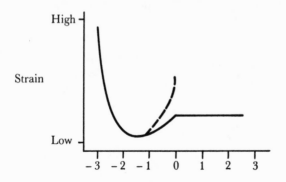

A. One-directional Models

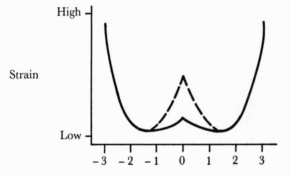

B. Two-directional Symmetrical Models

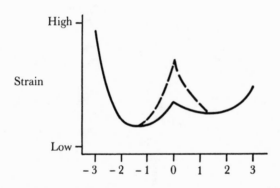

C. Two-directional Asymmetric Models

―――― Continuous

― ― ― Non-Continuous

guished according to the level of outcome hypothesized for perfect fit. Models based on adaptation level theory (Helson, 1964) generally assume *indifferent* effects for complete congruence, but Kahana (1978) suggests that, for dimensions other than stimulation, *negative* effects of perfect fit are more likely (as suggested by the dotted lines in Figure 4).

Overall, while the typology used here is hardly exhaustive, its description should suggest that the number of plausible quantitative models of person-environment congruence is far greater than that generally implied in the research literature. By highlighting such differences I hope to demonstrate that "the concept of person-environment fit is not as simple and straightforward as it may appear upon cursory examination. Correlation coefficients and assumptions of linear relationships between fit and behavior simply may not do justice to this complex interaction" (Hall, 1970, p. 212). In practice, of course, methods of measurement in the social sciences may not yet be precise enough to distinguish in a definitive way among the functional relationships suggested here, especially since linear relationships will typically account for most of the variance in measures which are at least *monotonically* related, whether linear or nonlinear (Nunnally, 1967). Precisely *because* our data are generally relatively crude and inadequate, however, more sophisticated theoretical, methodological, and statistical approaches are called for in their conceptualization and analysis (Wainer, 1978, p. 272).

Congruence Along Multiple Dimensions. Since the assessment of P-E fit in a given setting usually requires the measurement of a fairly comprehensive set of separate dimensions, an important question arises as to how, or whether, these separate dimensions should be combined in order to obtain an adequate representation of the degree of "total" fit for each individual. Kahana (1978) has suggested four general ways of deriving such an overall index of P-E fit, but each has important limitations. First, to derive a *simple* index of "total fit," one might focus exclusively on the total number of incongruent dimensions. Although readily quantifiable and parsimonious, this simple enumeration technique assumes somewhat naively that P-E relationships can be readily dichotomized as congruent or incongruent for each dimension. It also accentuates the *extensivity* of poorness-of-fit across dimensions while de-emphasizing *intensity* or degree of incongruence (Feldman, 1972).

A second approach seeks to include both the extent and intensity of incongruence by focusing on *cumulative mismatch* across dimensions. Measures of the degree of P-E discrepancy, signed or unsigned, are summed or averaged over all dimensions to yield a cumulative incongruence score. Reliance on such cumulative global indices may be faulted on at least two grounds: (1) an observed effect may be interpreted as general overall content of the index when it is actually due to one or two prominent dimensions; and (2) due to either mathematical or substantive cancellations across dimensions, such cumulative combinations may obscure or overlook significant relationships that exist in the data (Cronbach, 1958).

A third approach to combining measures of fit assumes that all areas of incongruence are not equally important, that even large discrepancies may be tolerated along less *salient dimensions*, while degree of incongruence in salient content areas can be especially crucial. While the logic of weighting congruence dimensions by importance before summing across dimensions is both conceptually elegant and logically appealing, a considerable body of research on the impact of differential weighting procedures on reliability and predictive power suggests that the approach will yield disappointing results (Mikes and Hulin, 1968; Wainer, 1976). Instead, techniques which take a more "ipsative" approach (Bem and Allen, 1974) to the assessment of incongruence along salient dimensions will probably be more successful.

Finally, several dimensions of congruence or fit may be dealt with by focusing on *profiles* of mismatch or incongruence; however, the *analytic* (as opposed to descriptive) treatment of congruence scores as profile data is also fraught with many potential hazards, since profiles generally yield three basic types of information—level or elevation (such as mean), dispersion or scatter (for instance, range or standard deviation), and shape (as for example, rank order)—each of which requires attention if one is to avoid violating certain underlying assumptions (Cronbach, 1958; Cronbach and Gleser, 1953; Nunnally, 1962). Several methods proposed for the study of P-E fit are, in fact, essentially measures of profile similarity (Cronbach and Gleser, 1953; Nunnally, 1962), whereby commensurate dimensions of P and E are conceived as two profiles of scores to be compared. Unfortunately, some of the measures proposed confound in one measure the three profile components noted above (Hall, 1970; Pervin, 1967), while others emphasize one component at the expense of the other two (Feather, 1972; Pelz and Andrews, 1966).

Conclusion

In this chapter I have described a general theory and method of person-situation interaction which emphasizes the interrelationship between the person and the environment, and the complex processes which underlie this relationship, by focusing on the goodness-of-fit between characteristics of the person and properties of the environment(s) to which he or she is commonly exposed. In doing so, models of person-environment congruence essentially make explicit and formalize the "matching" relationship between the person and environment, which is inherent in many general explanations of person-environment interaction, while also specifying and extending ideas which many interactionist theorists and researchers have already been using at an intuitive level for some time. By highlighting some of the basic advantages and limitations of conceiving of interactions as person-environment congruence, I hope to encourage more extensive and creative use of this approach, while also alerting potential practitioners to a broad array of complex conceptual and methodological issues associated with adopting the congruence or fit perspective.

References

Bem, D. J., and Allen, A. "On Predicting Some of the People Some of the Time: The Search for Cross-Situational Consistencies in Behavior." *Psychological Review*, 1974, *81*, 506–520.

Bereiter, C. "Some Persisting Dilemmas in the Measurement of Change." In C. W. Harris (Ed.), *Problems of Measuring Change*. Madison: University of Wisconsin Press, 1963.

Blau, P. M., and Duncan, O. D. *The American Occupational Structure*. New York: Wiley, 1967.

Bohrnstedt, G. W. "Observations on the Measurement of Change." In E. F. Borgatta and G. W. Bohrnstedt (Eds.), *Sociological Methodology 1969*. San Francisco: Jossey-Bass, 1969.

Caplan, R. D., and others. *Job Demands and Worker Health: Main Effects and Occupational Differences* (USGPO Catalog No. HE 20.7111:J57. USGPO Stock No. 1733-00083). Washington, D.C.: U.S. Government Printing Office, 1975.

Chayes, F. *Ratio Correlation*. Chicago: University of Chicago Press, 1971.

Cronbach, L. J. "Proposals Leading to the Analytic Treatment of Social Perception Scores." In R. Tagiuri and L. Petrullo (Eds.), *Person Perception and Interpersonal Behavior*. Stanford, Calif.: Stanford University Press, 1958.

Cronbach, L. J., and Furby, L. "How We Should Measure 'Change'—Or Should We?" *Psychological Bulletin*, 1970, *74*, 68–80.

Cronbach, L. J., and Gleser, G. "Assessing Similarity Between Profiles." *Psychological Bulletin*, 1953, *50*, 456–473.

Ekehammer, B. "Interactionism in Personality from a Historical Perspective. *Psychological Bulletin*, 1974, *81* (12), 1026–1048.

Feather, N. T. "Value Similarity and School Adjustment." *Australian Journal of Psychology*, 1972, *24* (2), 193–208.

Feather, N. T. *Values in Education and Society*. New York: Free Press, 1975.

Feldman, K. A. "Difficulties in Measuring and Interpreting Change and Stability During College." In K. A. Feldman (Ed.), *College and Student*. New York: Pergamon Press, 1972.

Feldman, K. A., and Newcomb, T. M. *The Impact of College on Students*. Vol. 1. San Francisco: Jossey-Bass, 1969.

French, Jr., J. R. P., and Kahn, R. L. "A Programmatic Approach to Studying the Industrial Environment and Mental Health." *Journal of Social Issues*, 1962, *18* (3), 1–47.

French, Jr., J. R. P., Rodgers, W., and Cobb, S. "Adjustment as Person-Environment Fit." In G. V. Coelho, D. A. Hamburg, and J. E. Adams (Eds.), *Coping and Adaptation*. New York: Basic Books, 1974.

Fuguitt, G. V., and Lieberson, S. "Correlation of Ratios or Difference Scores Having Common Terms." In H. Costner (Ed.), *Sociological Methodology 1973-1974*. San Francisco: Jossey-Bass, 1974.

70

Getzels, J. W. "The Social Psychology of Education." In G. Lindzey and E. Aronson (Eds.), *Handbook of Social Psychology.* Vol. 5 (2nd ed.). Reading, Mass.: Addison-Wesley, 1969.

Graham, W. K. "Commensurate Characteristics of Persons, Groups, and Organizations: Development of the Trait Ascription Questionnaire (TAQ)." *Human Relations,* 1976, *29* (7), 607–622.

Hackman, J. R., and Lawler, E. E., III. "Employee Reactions to Job Characteristics." *Journal of Applied Psychology Monograph,* 1971, *55,* 259–286.

Hall, D. T. "The Effect of Teacher-Student Congruence Upon Student Learning in College Classes." *Journal of Educational Psychology,* 1970, *61* (3), 205–213.

Harris, R. J. "The Uncertain Connection Between Verbal Theories and Research Hypotheses in Social Psychology." *Journal of Experimental Social Psychology,* 1976, *12* (2), 194–209.

Harrison, R. V. "Job Demands and Worker Health: Person-Environment Misfit." (Doctoral dissertation, University of Michigan, 1976). *Dissertation Abstracts International,* 1976, *37,* 1035B.

Harrison, R. V. "Person-Environment Fit and Job Stress." In C. L. Cooper and R. Payne (Eds.), *Stress at Work.* New York: Wiley, 1978.

Helson, H. *Adaptation-Level Theory: An Experimental and Systematic Approach to Behavior.* New York: Harper and Row, 1964.

Holland, J. L. *Making Vocational Choices: A Theory of Career.* Englewood Cliffs, N.J.: Prentice-Hall, 1973.

Imparato, N. "Relationships Between Porter's Need Satisfaction Questionnaire and the Job Descriptive Index." *Journal of Applied Psychology,* 1972, *56,* 397–405.

Jenkins, G. D., and others. "Standardized Observations: An Approach to Measuring the Nature of Jobs." *Journal of Applied Psychology,* 1975, *60* (2), 171–181.

Jorgenson, G. W. "Relationship of Classroom Behavior to the Accuracy of Match Between Material Difficulty and Student Ability." *Journal of Educational Psychology,* 1977, *69* (1), 24–32.

Kahana, E. "A Congruence Model of Person-Environment Interaction." In M. P. Lawton (Ed.), *Theory Development in Environments and Aging.* New York: Wiley, 1978.

Kessler, R. C. "The Use of Change Scores as Criteria in Longitudinal Survey Research." *Quality and Quantity,* 1977, *11* (1), 43–66.

Kulka, R. A. "Person-Environment Fit in the High School: A Validation Study." 2 vols. (Doctoral dissertation, The University of Michigan, 1975). *Dissertation Abstracts International,* 1976, *36,* 5352B.

Kulka, R. A., Klingel, D. M., and Mann, D. W. "Dimensions of Student-School Fit as Predictors of School Crime and Disruption." Paper presented at the Annual Meeting of the Society for the Study of Social Problems, San Francisco, September 1978.

Kulka, R. A., Mann, D. W., and Klingel, D. M. "School Crime as a Function of Person-Environment Fit." In National Council on Crime and Delinquency (Ed.), *Theoretical Perspectives on Poverty and School Crime.* Unpublished report to the U.S. Department of Health, Education, and Welfare, 1978.

Lawler, E. E., III. *Motivation in Work Organizations.* Belmont, Calif.: Wadsworth Publishing Co., 1973.

Lewin, K. *Field Theory in Social Science.* (D. Cartwright, Ed.). New York: Harper and Row, 1951.

Locke, E. A. "What Is Job Satisfaction?" *Organizational Behavior and Human Performance,* 1969, *4,* 309–336.

Lord, F. M. "Elementary Models for Measuring Change." In C. W. Harris (Ed.), *Problems in Measuring Change.* Madison: University of Wisconsin Press, 1963.

Marks, E. "Personality and Motivational Factors in Response to an Environmental Description Scale." *Journal of Educational Psychology,* 1968, *59,* 267–274.

Mikes, P. S., and Hulin, C. L. "Use of Importance as a Weighting Component of Job Satisfaction." *Journal of Applied Psychology,* 1968, *52,* 394–398.

Moos, R. *Evaluating Treatment Environments: A Social Ecological Approach.* New York: Wiley, 1974.

Nunnally, J. C. "The Analysis of Profile Data." *Psychological Bulletin,* 1962, *59,* 311–319.

Nunnally, J. C. *Psychometric Theory.* New York: McGraw-Hill, 1967.

Olweus, D. "A Critical Analysis of the 'Modern' Interactionist Position." In D. Magnusson and N. S. Endler (Eds.), *Personality at the Crossroads: Current Issues in Interactional Psychology.* Hillsdale, N.J.: Erlbaum, 1977.

Pelz, D. C., and Andrews, F. M. *Scientists in Organizations.* New York: Wiley, 1966.

Pervin, L. A. "A Twenty-College Study of Student X College Interaction Using TAPE (Transactional Analysis of Personality and Environment): Rationale, Reliability, and Validity." *Journal of Educational Psychology,* 1967, *58,* 290–302.

Pervin, L. A. "Performance and Satisfaction as a Function of Individual-Environment Fit." *Psychological Bulletin,* 1968, *69* (1), 56–68.

Robinson, W. S. "The Statistical Measurement of Agreement." *American Sociological Review,* 1957, *22,* 17–25.

Schneider, B., and Bartlett, C. J. "Individual Differences and Organizational Climate II: Measurement of Organizational Climate by the Multi-Trait, Multi-Rater Matrix." *Personnel Psychology,* 1970, *23,* 493–512.

Schuessler, K. "Analysis of Ratio Variables: Opportunities and Pitfalls." *American Journal of Sociology,* 1974, *80* (2), 379–396.

Southwood, K. E. "Substantive Theory and Statistical Interaction: Five Models." *American Journal of Sociology,* 1978, *83* (5), 1154–1203.

Stern, G. *People in Context: Measuring Person-Environment Congruence in Education and Industry.* New York: Wiley, 1970.

Veroff, J., and Feld, S. *Marriage and Work in America.* New York: Van Nostrand Reinhold, 1970.

Wainer, H. "Estimating Coefficients in Linear Models: It Don't Make No Nevermind." *Psychological Bulletin,* 1976, *83,* 213–217.

Wainer, H. "On the Sensitivity of Regression and Regressors." *Psychological Bulletin,* 1978, *85* (2), 267–273.

Wylie, R. C. *The Self-Concept: A Review of Methodological Considerations and Measuring Instruments.* Lincoln: University of Nebraska Press, 1974.

Richard A. Kulka is an assistant research scientist with the Institute for Social Research at The University of Michigan.

The relationships among traits, situations, and behavior
are analyzed in the context of behavioral criterion measures.

Personality and Behavioral Prediction: An Analysis of Behavioral Criterion Measures

James Jaccard

The trait concept in psychology has been the subject of considerable controversy in recent years. Traits have traditionally been conceptualized as relatively stable and broad dispositions that influence an individual's behavior. Mischel (1968) and others (Peterson, 1968) have criticized the trait approach to behavioral analysis and suggested that alternative theories and research models are necessary. This has led to the development of perspectives such as situationism (Mischel, 1968, 1973, 1976) and interactionism (Bowers, 1973; Endler, 1973, 1976; Magnusson and Endler, 1977).

Criticisms of the trait construct have typically focused on three arguments (Block, 1977): (1) Indicators and measures of traits generally exhibit little consistency across time and situations; hence one can question whether these indicators reflect "stable and broad" dispositions; (2) traits are largely constructs of the observer rather than of independent information about the individual's actual behavior; and (3) inferences from traits exhibit little predictive utility. Each of these arguments has stimulated considerable empirical research. Some investigators have concluded that the results tend to support the validity of the arguments (Mischel, 1968), while others have reached an opposite or at least more guarded conclusion (Block, 1977).

The thesis of the present chapter is quite simple. The concept of trait must be evaluated, in large part, on its ability to help us understand and predict behavior. This requires three considerations: (1) a careful analysis of our conceptualization and operationalization of *traits,* (2) a careful analysis of our conceptualization and operationalization of *behaviors* and (3) a careful analysis of their relationships in the context of a theoretical network. Since our goal is ultimately to understand and predict behavior, a logical starting point is the analysis of types of behavioral criterion measures an investigator may wish to predict and understand.

Taxonomy of Behavioral Measures

At the simplest level, a behavioral observation can be made at a single point in time with respect to one behavior, that is, a *single act, single observation* measure. This measure may be conceptualized as a cell in a two dimensional table that has repeated observations as columns and different behaviors as rows (Fishbein, 1973). Table 1 presents such a matrix. The rows represent those behaviors that the theorist believes are related to the trait dimension in question or that are viewed as being theoretically tied to one another (for "aggressiveness" the behaviors might be "insulting an individual" and "physically assaulting an individual"). The occasions represent periods of observation as defined by the investigator (for instance, p = 15 minute intervals, p = daily observations, p = trials).

Table 1. Types of Behavioral Measures

		Occasions					
		1	*2*	. . . .		*P*	
Behaviors	1	$b_{1,1}$	$b_{1,2}$	. . . . .	. . . . .	$b_{1,b}$	R_1
	2	$b_{2,1}$	$b_{2,2}$	. . . . .	. . . . .	$b_{2,p}$	R_2
	:	:	:	:	:	:	:
	:	:	:	:	:	:	:
	:	:	:	:	:	:	:
	m	$b_{m,1}$	$b_{m,2}$	. . . . .	. . . . .	$b_{m,p}$	R_m
		M_1	M_2	. . . .		M_p	

Table 1 suggests a number of behavioral measures other than the single act, single observation criterion that can potentially be predicted from indices of personality traits. First, the *single act, repeated observation* (R_i) measure is based on the row marginal for a given behavior. For example, the occurrence or nonoccurrence of a behavior could be noted at each of five observation periods. This results in a 1×5 matrix with a behavioral score in each cell. A single act, repeated observation measure would involve combining the behavioral scores for the five observation periods to derive an overall, repeated observation score (R_i).

A second behavioral criterion measure is a *multiple act* measure based on a given column marginal for a set of behaviors (M_i). This measure takes into account different behaviors, each observed during a given occasion. The emphasis here is not on the performance or nonperformance of a single behavior, but rather on the observation of a *behavioral pattern*. A third type of measure, a *multiple act, repeated observation* behavioral criterion, is derived by combining either the column marginals (M_i) or row marginals (R_i) into one overall index (MR). This description of repeated observation and multiple act measures does not specify how to obtain the actual criterion scores. Entries in cells can be combined in very different ways (such as, summed or weighted sum of scores). For this reason, a multiple act repeated observation score based on the R_i may be quite different from one based on the M_i.

It is possible, then, to specify four major classes of behavioral measures, (1) single act, single observation measures, (2) single act, repeated observation measures, (3) multiple act measures, and (4) multiple act, repeated observation measures. Within each class, subclasses of measures can also be specified. For example, a score in a given cell of the behavioral matrix can be either dichotomous (whether or not a person donates money to a given charity, for instance) or continuous (how much money a person donates to a given charity). Thus, one can distinguish between *single dichotomous act, single observation* behavioral measures and *single continuous act, single observation* behavioral measures. With respect to behavioral measures involving repeated observations, the repeated observations can be made under a number of different conditions. On the one hand, the repeated observations can be made under maximally *homogeneous* conditions, whereby situational and environmental variables are held constant across observation periods. Under such conditions one would be measuring, in part, the *reliability* of the behavior. On the other hand, the repeated observations can be made under maximally *heterogeneous* conditions whereby situational and environmental variables are systematically varied across observation periods. Under such conditions one would be measuring, in part, the *generalizabil-*

ity of the behavior. Thus it is also possible to specify behavioral measures such as *single act, repeated observations under homogeneous conditions* as well as *single act, repeated observations under heterogeneous conditions,* and so on.

Some general points should be made: First, behavioral observations are but one kind of data utilized by social scientists. Just as other types of data are measured, coded, quantified, or categorized, so are behavioral observations. As McGrath (1964) has noted, data are nothing more than "coded records of selected aspects of behavior." Behavioral observations that are used to validate personality measures or to test for a relation between a given trait and behavior are therefore susceptible to similar types of measurement errors and thereby require the same degree of scrutiny that these other "psychological" variables receive.

Second, the strategy and types of variables one considers in attempting to predict and understand behavior will depend upon the type of behavioral criterion measure one is trying to predict and understand. For example, personality traits have typically been defined as broad, underlying dispositions that influence behaviors of individuals across situations. Such variables would therefore seem best suited to the prediction and understanding of behavioral patterns as operationalized by multiple act measures or multiple act, repeated observation measures. It is unfortunate, then, that most studies evaluating the predictive utility of traits focus on single act behavioral measures.

Third, although traits have typically been defined as predispositions, the exact nature of this disposition has usually been left ambiguous. Dispositions are often inferred from behavioral observations and, as such, the above taxonomy makes explicit different ways of conceptualizing a disposition. On the simplest and most specific level, one can speak of a disposition to perform a specific behavior in a specific situation. This would correspond to a single act, single observation behavioral measure and does not typify trait conceptualizations. A single act, repeated observation measure would imply a more general predisposition. The individual is disposed to perform a specific behavior. On some occasions the individual will perform the behavior, while on other occasions he or she will not. Across a number of occasions (observations), however, individuals with greater degrees of the trait will be more likely to perform the behavior than individuals with lesser degrees of the trait (the marginal R score will be greater for high versus low individuals on the trait dimension in question). A multiple act measure implies an even more general predisposition. With this type of behavioral measure an individual may or may not perform a given behavior on a given occasion. Across multiple behaviors, however, the individual will tend to exhibit a *behavioral pattern* that reflects the trait in question. Two individuals may have equal degrees of the disposition in question (equal M scores) but exhibit different behaviors with respect to that dimension (one individual may perform behaviors 1, 2, and 6 in a multiple act behavioral score, whereas the other may perform behaviors 3, 4, and 5). In this respect, an individual may be disposed to exhibit a certain *degree* of the trait dimension (such as dominance) in a behavioral pattern rather than being disposed to perform specific behaviors.

It is possible to derive a number of additional conceptualizations of dispositions based on the other types of behavioral criteria or methods of combining behavioral scores. The optimal conceptualization of trait as a disposition obviously depends upon the purposes for which an investigator wants to use that concept. It does seem clear, however, that current conceptualizations of traits imply rather general dispositions as characterized by multiple act and multiple act, repeated observation measures. For a further discussion of this issue, see Jaccard (1974).

Once an investigator has made explicit his or her conceptualization of a trait, the task then becomes one of developing a measure of that trait for purposes of testing theoretical relationships between the trait and other concepts and behavior. Block (1977) and others (Wiggins, 1973) have reviewed procedures for constructing such measures. It is useful at this point to reiterate three points made by Block concerning personality concepts:

"1. Many concepts have not been well represented by their operational indicators. Psychologists have been extraordinarily casual and even irresponsible in developing measures to represent concepts. In coordinating a concept with a measure, it is incumbent on the psychologist to justify, via construct validation, the propriety of this assigned correspondence . . . .

2. Behavioral hypotheses derived from concepts should reflect the complexity and the implications of the concept being studied. Concepts have to be thought about; they often have complicated or contingent or interactive implications that should be but are not respected in psychological research . . .

3. The reliability of many of the measures employed in personality research and the power of the research designs employed is often poor, unnecessarily so. It makes no sense to use measures so unreliable that subsequent intercorrelations among measures are constrained to be close to zero. It is also unreasonable to interpret research, by oneself or by others, when the reliabilities of the measures used [are] unknown or not taken into account" (Block, 1977, p. 40).

The remainder of this chapter will focus on the role of personality traits in the prediction and understanding of one type of behavioral criterion, namely single dichotomous act, single observation behaviors. The decision to focus discussion on this type of criterion may seem inappropriate given the comments made about traits and multiple act criteria. However, there are several reasons for considering single instead of multiple act criteria. (Hereafter, the term "single act criterion" will always refer to single dichotomous act, single observation behavioral measures.) First, a large number of studies on the trait-behavior relationship have used single act criterion measures. On the basis of this research, one would be inclined to question seriously the utility of traits in the understanding and prediction of single act criteria. On the contrary, personality traits can be useful in the prediction and understanding of these behaviors. In order to see this, however, it is necessary to place the concept of trait into a theoretical framework of behavioral prediction. Such a framework will be outlined and its relationship to situationism and interactionism briefly considered. Second, a large number of important behaviors can be conceptualized as single act, single observation criteria. These would include behaviors related to such areas as politics, altruism, population growth, aggression, health, and job performance. A framework for predicting and understanding such behaviors would be of obvious utility. For a brief discussion of the relationship between traits and multiple act criteria, see Jaccard (1974). In the discussion that follows, traits will be conceptualized as general predispositions, similar to that outlined in the context of multiple act criteria and consistent with most current conceptualizations of traits. In addition, it will be assumed that reliable and valid measures of traits have been developed that are consistent with this conceptualization.

Prediction of Single Act Criteria. The present paper outlines a general theory for the prediction of single act criteria. In doing so, it is explicitly recognized that modifications of the theory may be called for as it is applied to specific content areas. Further, the theory is not applicable to all of the types of behaviors that have been studied in the context of personality. Nevertheless, it should have relatively general applicability to many behaviors of interest to social scientists. By no means is the theory to be presented completely new and/or original. Rather, it represents basic ideas that have been discussed in several research areas including attitude theory (Fishbein, 1967; Triandis, 1977), decision theory (Edwards, 1954; Lee, 1971), and social judgment theory. Some modifications and extensions of these ideas have, however, been made.

Researchers have emphasized the fact that both situational and personality variables can influence an individual's behavior at a given point in time. The present theory develops the general perspective that individuals behave on the basis of how they *interpret* different aspects of the situation in which they find themselves. Manipulation of situational variables will influence the kinds of cognitions an individual forms. Similarly, the individual's past experience and personality will influence the kinds of cognitions one forms (how one interprets the situation). Further, these variables may interact to influence cognitions. In order to fully understand the influence of personality and situational variables on behavior, a theory which specifies the more immediate *psychological* determinants of behavior must be developed. In this manner, the effects of individual differences and manipulation of situational variables can be mapped through the theoretical network to understand more fully the relationship (or lack of relationship) between these variables and behavior.

Decisions and Behavioral Performance. The *prediction* of many social behaviors can be a rather simple and straightforward matter. If one wants to know whether or not an individual will perform a given behavior (vote for a politician, attend a clinic, or use birth control), probably the most efficient strategy is to ask the individual if he or she intends to perform that behavior. An affirmative response would lead to the prediction of behavioral performance, whereas a negative response would lead to the prediction of non-performance.

Such a statement of behavioral intent can be viewed as a decision on the part of an individual to perform or not to perform a behavior. In general, such decisions will be very predictive of behavioral performance, as numerous studies have demonstrated (Dulany, 1968; Fishbein and Jaccard, 1973; Jaccard, Knox, and Brinberg, in press). However, once an individual has decided to perform a behavior, this does not guarantee performance of that behavior. A number of factors can influence the extent to which one can predict a measure of behavior from a measure of the individual's behavioral decision. These factors can be classified into two groups: (1) those pertaining to measurement issues and (2) those that directly moderate the relationship between the behavioral decision and behavior.

Measurement Issues. One factor influencing the prediction of behavior from a measure of the individual's behavioral decision is the *time interval* between the measurement of the decision and the observation of the behavior. In general, as the time interval between these two measures increases, the relationship between them can be expected to decrease. This phenomenon has been observed in a number of social psychological studies (Westoff, Mishler, and Kelly, 1957). Obviously, it is not the passage of time per se that influences the relationship between the decision measure and behavior. Rather, some event must occur during the time interval that either changes the individual's decision or renders behavioral performance impossible. During this interval the individuals may be exposed to new information causing them to alter their decision. The resultant behavior should reflect this new decision as opposed to the old one.

A second measurement problem concerns the specificity of the measured behavioral decision and the behavioral criterion. If the behavioral criterion concerns a specific behavior to be performed in a specific place at a specific time, then the corresponding decision measure should refer to behavioral performance at that place and that time. More precisely, a behavioral criterion consists of four elements: an *action,* the *object* the action is directed toward, the *situation* in which the action is to be performed, and the *time* at which the action occurs. Each of these elements differs on a dimension of specificity. At the most specific level, a person can perform a particular action with respect to a given object in a specified situation at a given point in time. More general levels involve greater abstraction on the respective dimension. With respect to time, for example, the behavioral criterion can refer to a given point in time (2 o'clock this afternoon), a specified time period (the week of May 20th) or an unlimited time period (during the person's lifetime). Once an investigator has established a behavioral criterion, he or she has (either implicitly or explicitly) defined the levels of specificity of the four elements. The most predictive behavioral decision measure should be that measure which is correspondent with these specific levels. As the level of specificity of the behavior deviates from that of the decision measure, the observed relation between these measures can be expected to decrease (Fishbein, 1966; Hornik, 1970). Although this point may seem obvious, its implications frequently have been ignored.

A third measurement problem concerns the degree to which the individual's stated behavioral decision represents a true behavioral decision. Obviously, if persons mislead an investigator regarding their true intent, there will be little relationship between the measured behavioral decision and behavior. A researcher must therefore use all possible means for ensuring that persons report their true decision.

Intervening Factors. A number of variables directly influence the relationship between a decision to perform a behavior and behavioral performance. One such factor is the number of behaviors or "steps" the individual must perform before he or she can enact the behavioral criterion. For example, in order to donate blood a person must (1) learn where he or she can go to donate blood, (2) make an appointment, (3) arrange transportation to the appointment site, (4) arrive at the blood bank, (5) pass a physical, and (6) give blood. Different behaviors may require different numbers of steps leading to performance of that behavior. As the number of steps increases, the correspondence between the behavioral decision and overt behavior might decrease, especially when performance of one or more of the steps is dependent upon some other person or event.

A number of approaches to behavioral prediction may be derived from the above. First, a quantitative measure of the behavioral decision can be obtained. This measure should indicate the likelihood that the individual will initiate the first step toward the behavior. The higher the person's score on this measure, the more likely it is he or she will advance along the behavioral sequence of steps and complete the behavioral act. Second, it may be possible to develop a stochastic model to describe the behavioral sequence. Probabilities for the initial stage of the sequence could be obtained by ascertaining the behavioral decisions, while probabilities at each subsequent stage would be derived retrospectively from group data on the different behavioral steps.

Additional variables that influence the decision-behavior relationship can be specified. One such variable is *ability*. A decision to perform a behavior is merely that — a decision. If the individual does not have the ability to perform the behavior, then the decision will not result in behavioral performance. An individual may intend to throw a football 300 yards, but lack the necessary ability.

A second moderator variable is *habit*. An individual may decide to perform a behavior (drive a new route to work, for instance), but, by force of habit, unconsciously performs an alternative one (drive the regular route to work). A third moderator variable focuses on *memory*. Often times an individual will decide to perform a behavior on a given occasion but accidently forget when the occasion occurs (a person may intend to donate blood at an upcoming drive but forget about the drive on the days it is held).

To summarize, many behaviors of concern to social scientists are volitional in nature and hence can be accurately predicted from measures of behavioral decisions. Numerous studies have observed strong relations between such measures and behavior. However, prediction of behavior from decision measures may be reduced by a number of factors which must be taken into account to improve behavioral prediction. This will especially be true when there is a long time interval between measurement of the decision and observation of the behavior, when performance of the behavior can only occur following some sequence of behaviors, and when these sequenced behaviors depend upon other people or events.

A major focus of the present theory of social behavior, then, is on the relationship between behavioral decisions and behavior, along with specification of variables that can affect this relationship. The above discussion has important implications for understanding the relationship among situational variables, measures of personality traits, and single act behavioral measures. Let us first consider personality traits. First, many traits can influence the type of behavioral decisions an individual makes. For example, individuals who tend to be "sociable" may be more likely to decide to attend a social meeting than those who tend to be unsociable. However, if this behavioral decision is not manifested into behavioral performance, a low relationship between measures of sociability and attendance at the meeting would be observed. Certain personality traits may relate systematically to *behavioral decisions,* but not to actual behavior, due to the moderating effects of such variables as ability, habit, dependency upon others, or time. Accordingly, the relationship between traits and single act behavioral measures can be better understood by taking these moderator variables into account.

Over and above this, certain personality traits may also be useful as moderator variables with respect to the relationship between behavioral decisions and behavior. For example, one factor that influences behavioral predictability is the time interval between the measurement of the behavioral decision and behavioral observation. During this interval, the individual might change his or her intention and decide not to perform the behavior. Certain types of individuals may be more likely to change their behavioral decisions (and hence be incorrectly predicted), whereas other individuals may be more likely to maintain stable behavioral decisions (and hence be correctly predicted). Measures of personality traits might be able to capture these individual differences and lead to improved behavioral predictability.

In terms of situational variables, the same considerations apply. Manipulation of a situational variable may have a strong effect on a person's decision to perform a behavior. However, systematic relationships between these manipulations and behavioral performance may not be observed due to the moderating effects of variables such as ability or time. Research studying the relationship between situational variables, personality variables and behavior could profit by incorporating the notion of behavioral decisions and factors that influence the relationship between decisions and actual behavioral performance.

The relation between behavioral decisions and actual behavior is an important one and additional research is needed on variables that moderate this relationship. An equally important question concerns the specification of variables that influence a behavioral decision: How does an individual decide to perform or not perform a behavior? Although a detailed consideration of this problem is well beyond the scope of this chapter, a general framework that specifies the immediate social psychological determinants of behavioral decisions will be briefly considered. The utility of personality traits and a situational analysis within this framework will then be made explicit.

Determinants of Behavioral Decisions. The present theory is concerned with situations in which an individual has an opportunity to perform one of n alternate behaviors, $B_1, B_2, \ldots B_n$. These behaviors must be mutually exclusive and exhaustive, such that performance of one precludes performance of another. On the simplest level, one can always speak of two behavioral alternatives, (1) performing the behavior (such as signing a petition) and (2) not performing that behavior (not signing a petition). Associated with each alternative are two classes of variables (1) *personal* considerations and (2) *normative* considerations. Personal considerations are typically associated with a person's attitude toward the behavioral alternative in question. Specifically, they refer to the perceived advantages and disadvantages of performing the alternative. Any given perceived advantage or disadvantage has two components. First, the *certainty* component refers to how certain the individual is that performance of the alternative will, in fact, lead to the advantage or disadvantage in question. Second, the *evaluative* component refers to the *degree* to which the advantage is positively valued (very, moderately, or slightly) or the *degree* to which the disadvantage is negatively valued (very, moderately, or slightly). In general, if an individual is certain that the behavioral alternative will lead to highly positive outcomes, then the individual will have a positive attitude toward that alternative. If an individual is certain that the behavioral alternative will lead to highly negative outcomes, then the individual will have a negative attitude toward that alternative. Several theorists (Fishbein, 1963; Rosenberg, 1956) have specified precise relationships regarding how the certainty and evaluative components combine to influence the attitude toward the alternative in question.

Normative considerations draw from sociological theory where behavior is viewed as being determined by norms. In the present theory, following Fishbein (1967), a norm is conceptualized as a *perception* by an individual that a given referent (parent, close friend) thinks he or she should or should not perform the behavioral alternative in question. A given norm also has two components. First, a *normative strength* component refers to the degree and direction of the perceived norm (that is, perceptions as to whether a referent thinks the individual should or should not perform the alternative in question and how strongly the referent feels about this). Second, the *referent importance* component refers to how important the referent is to the individual. In general, if an individual perceives that important referents oppose performance of the alternative, the individual will experience strong normative pressure not to perform that alternative. If an individual perceives that important referents favor performance of the alternative, the individual will experience strong normative pressure to perform that alternative. Fishbein (1967) has suggested one type of relationship for combining variables similar to these two normative components.

For each behavioral alternative, an individual possesses an attitude toward performing that alternative (personal considerations) as well as normative pressures (normative considerations) to perform or not perform that alternative. These factors will ultimately determine the decision a person makes. There will probably be individual differences in the relative contributions of personal versus normative considerations in making a behavioral decision. For example, some individuals might only consider personal factors. Research in decision theory would suggest that such individuals will perform the behavioral alternative toward which the most positive attitude is held. Other individuals might only consider normative factors. It can be suggested that such individuals will perform the behavioral alternative toward which the strongest normative pressures are perceived (with regard to performing that behavior). Finally, other individuals may consider both personal and normative factors in making a behavioral decision. When the attitudes and perceived norms are consistent with one another, prediction of the behavioral decision would follow from either of the two principles stated above. However, when the distribution of attitudes across behavioral alternatives differs from the distribution of normative pressures, these individuals will experience conflict and must resolve this conflict in some fashion.

Personality traits can potentially be utilized to good effect in the above theoretical framework. First, there may be personality correlates of individual differences with respect to the relative importance of attitudinal versus normative considerations in determining the behavioral decision. One might hypothesize that on an internality-externality dimension (Rotter, 1975), internals are more likely to consider attitudinal factors whereas externals are more likely to consider normative factors. Similar predictions can be derived for a number of trait dimensions (for example, social desirability). Personality measures may thus help us understand behavioral decisions by providing insights into the weighting of attitudinal versus normative considerations. Second, personality measures may provide insights into the types of advantages/disadvantages or normative perceptions an individual may form and take into consideration in making a decision (people who are "sociable" may perceive very different types of advantages and disadvantages of "going to a party" than people who are "unsociable"). Third, personality measures may suggest specific change strategies when attempting to alter behavioral decisions. Specifically, personality differences could suggest the types of perceptions that would be most resistant to change as well as those that would be most susceptible to change.

Similar considerations apply in the context of situational variables. The manipulation of a situational variable may influence the relative importance of attitudinal versus normative considerations in determining the behavioral decision. A behavior that is to be performed in the presence as opposed to the absence of another may affect the salience of normative influences. Similarly, the manipulation of a situational variable may influence the kinds of advantages/disadvantages or normative perceptions an individual forms and takes into consideration in making a decision. By measuring these influences, the relationship (or lack of relationship) between situational variables and behavior might be better understood.

To summarize, both situational and personality variables can influence behavior. The effects of these variables on behavior will be mediated by the components of the theory outlined above. The manipulation of a situational variable may influence the perceived advantages and disadvantages of performing a given behavioral alternative. However, this manipulation may have no effect on behavior since the behavioral decision is determined by normative considerations and not personal considerations; or the manipulation of the situational variable may make more positive the attitude toward performing a given alternative, but it may not raise it to a level whereby it exceeds the attitude toward performing some other behavior (yielding no differences at the level of behavioral decision); or the situational manipulation may increase the attitude sufficiently, resulting in a change in the behavioral decision, but this manipulation may not be reflected in behavior due to the moderating effects of ability. And so on.

The potential utility of personality traits and situational variables for understanding and changing social behavior becomes more evident when such variables are placed in a theoretical framework. This includes the consideration of the relationship between behavioral decisions and behavior as well as the immediate social psychological determinants of behavioral decisions. The relationship between traits and single act criteria can best be understood in the context of such a framework.

Traits and the Prediction of Single Act Criteria. The above analysis briefly outlines a theoretical network for predicting and understanding single act behavioral criteria in which personality concepts can be investigated. Nevertheless, it still does not completely consider the issue of when single act criteria will be related to traditional measures of traits. The fact remains that correlations between traits and single act criteria are generally weak. The above analysis of the relationship between behavioral decisions and behavior should provide some answers to this question. However, even if behavioral decisions are substituted as the major dependent variable (instead of behavior), low correlations may still persist. One major reason that traits do not systematically relate to single act criteria is the obvious fact that situational variables (and their interaction with traits) can also influence behavior. However, an additional problem focuses upon the rather restricted model that has guided studies of the trait-behavior relationship. This model, and alternative ones, can be made explicit through scaling theory. The following discussion will assume strong correspondence between behavioral decisions and behavior and hence, circumvent consideration of variables that moderate this relationship.

Insights into the relationship between traits and behavior can be gained through the application and analysis of scaling theory used in the development of personality measures. An investigator generates a set of verbal items that he or she thinks measures the trait dimension in question, such as dominance. Individuals are asked to agree or disagree with each item and these responses are then scored for dominance. Items are then subjected to an item analysis, usually in the form of item-total correlations or factor analysis. Items that do not meet the standards set forth in such analyses are eliminated.

The use of item-total correlations (and factor analysis) assumes a specific type of relationship between responses to the verbal items and the person's true personality score. This relationship is known in scaling theory as the *traceline* of an item or an *item operating characteristic* (Green, 1954). Take, for example, an item for which endorsement would indicate dominance. The traceline of this item (the relationship between the probability of endorsing the item and the person's true personality score) would be positive, and linear if item-total correlations form the basis for the selection of items. The upper left panel of Figure 1 presents such a traceline. The underlying assumption is essentially that the more dominant the individual, the more likely it is the individual will endorse the item.

There is no reason, however, why other types of tracelines could not be assumed. In attitude scaling, for example, Thurstone procedures posit a very different type of traceline (Thurstone and Chave, 1929). Thurstone's method of equal-appearing intervals requires the following steps in scale construction: (1) the experimenter generates a pool of items deemed relevant to the attitude in question. These items should cover the entire affective dimension including favorable, neutral, and unfavorable responses. (2) The items are given to a set of judges who classify these along an 11 point unfavorable–favorable dimension as to the amount of favorability that endorsement of that item would reflect with respect to the attitude object. (3) The *criterion of ambiguity* (Thurstone and Chave, 1929) is applied and items that do not receive uniform favorability ratings are eliminated. (4) For the remain-

Figure 1. Theoretical Tracelines of Different Scaling Procedures

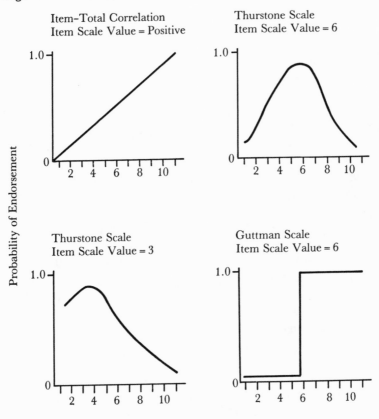

True Personality Score

ing items, a *scale value* for each item is derived. This value is typically the median favorability rating made by the judges, and can range from 1 to 11. Items with low scale values reflect negative affect with respect to the attitude object while items with high scale values reflect positive affect with respect to the attitude object. Ultimately, the final attitude score for a given individual will be determined by computing the average scale value of items the individual endorses. However, step 5 in scale construction involves the application of the *criterion of irrelevance*, which is directly related to the traceline of items assumed in Thurstone scaling. The basic assumption underlying the criterion of irrelevance is that an item with a given scale value is most likely to be endorsed by individuals whose true attitudes are located at the same position on the attitude dimension. The greater the discrepancy between the *person's* location on the dimension and the *item's* location (scale value) on that dimension, the lower the probability the person will endorse the item. The upper right panel in Figure 1 presents the traceline of an item whose scale value is 6 such that it meets the assumption of the criterion of irrelevance. It can be seen that this traceline is non-monotonic and is in sharp contrast to a linear traceline. The lower left panel presents a traceline for an item whose scale value is 3.

Thurstonian scaling procedures can readily be applied to the scaling of personality traits. For example, an investigator could generate verbal items that supposedly measure dominance. A set of judges could rate each item on an 11 point submissive-dominant scale in the same fashion as described earlier. Ambiguous items would be deleted and scale values for the remaining items computed. Further analyses would eliminate items that do not meet the criterion of irrelevance (see Summers, 1970, and Thurstone and Chave, 1929 for an elaboration of these procedures). The important point, however, is that the traceline assumed in Thurstone scaling is very different from one assumed with item-total or factor analytic procedures. An item with a scale value of 6 that meets the criterion of irrelevance would be rejected from a scale whose criterion for item retention is based on item-total correlations. This is because item-total correlations assume *linear* tracelines, whereas Thurstone scaling assumes non-monotonic tracelines (except for items with extreme values). Thus, the approaches differ in the presumed relationship between responses to items and the person's score on the trait dimension in question.

This rather long-winded exposition of tracelines is useful for understanding the trait-behavior relationship if one merely substitutes overt behaviors for verbal items on a personality scale. Instead of being concerned with the relationship between "probability of endorsement" and the true personality score, concern is now with "probability of behavioral performance" and its relationship to the true personality score. The item-total correlation procedure dictates that the more dominant the individual, the more likely it is the individual will perform the behavior. This line of reasoning is consistent with correlational studies of the trait-behavior relationship and typifies most research on this question. However, the logic of the Thurstone scale implies a very different type of psychological process. According to this perspective, behavioral prediction requires knowledge of the behavior's scale value on the trait dimension in question, namely dominance. Once this scale value is known, individuals whose true personality score is equal to this scale value should be most likely to perform the behavior. As the discrepancy between the person's true personality score and the behavior's scale value becomes greater, the probability of behavioral performance decreases. If this model is operative, then low *correlations* between trait indexes and behavioral performance would be expected since correlations measure the *linear* relationship between variables. Accurate behavioral prediction would require knowledge of the behavior's scale value and appropriate non-correlational statistics.

This state of affairs becomes even more intriguing if one applies other scaling techniques that assume tracelines different than the item-total correlation and Thurstone approaches. One example is Guttman scaling (1944) which assumes a step-shaped traceline, as illustrated in the lower right panel of Figure 1. Again, knowledge of a behavior's scale value is required. The assumed traceline would dictate the following: When the person's location on the trait dimension is lower than that of the scale value of the behavior, the probability the individual will perform the behavior is zero. When the person's location on the trait dimension is equal to or exceeds the scale value of the behavior, the probability of behavioral performance is 1.0. This is analogous to a threshold model and, again, produces a traceline that is nonlinear. Numerous other viable tracelines could be specified, although further consideration of this matter is beyond the scope of this chapter.

The major point is that studies that correlate measures of traits with measures of single act criteria assume a model whereby a linear relationship between these variables is posited. Such a viewpoint may be restrictive and other types of relationships may be involved. If an estimate of a behavior's scale value can be obtained, a number of plausible alternative psychological models can be specified (via the logic of Thurstone, Guttman, and others) that would, by definition, produce low trait-behavior correlations. Research concerning these alternative models is currently being conducted by the present author. Furthermore, not all behaviors may follow the same type of traceline. Some behaviors may have linear tracelines, while others may have Thurstonian tracelines, and so on. Variables that describe these behavioral differences are also being investigated.

In the context of the theory outlined in the previous section, the implications are straightforward. An individual difference variable may be related to behavior following a Thurstone type model. If the behavior's scale value is moderate, this would suggest that individuals with high or low scores on the trait dimension would not perform the behavior, whereas those with moderate scores should perform the behavior. These behavioral differences should be reflected in differential behavioral decisions and, in turn, different attitudes toward the behavioral alternatives and/or differences in perceptions of normative pressures. To be sure, people high on the dimension may differ in their reasons for not performing the behavior from those who score low on the dimension. However, these differences should be tractable through the theoretical network.

Summary and Conclusion

The understanding of the relationship between traits and behavior requires a careful analysis of behavioral criterion measures. A taxonomy of measures was presented and it was suggested that personality traits, as traditionally conceptualized, are best suited to the prediction of multiple act rather than single act criteria. With regard to single act criteria, the utility of traits and situational variables in understanding, predicting, and changing behavior can best be evaluated in the context of a theoretical framework. Such a framework was briefly presented. Finally, it was argued that the application of scaling theory to the analysis of the trait-behavior relationship could provide interesting insights into the prediction of single act criteria from measures of personality. Several alternative psychological models of this relationship were discussed. Most analyses of trait-behavior discrepancies have focused on the independent variable of the relationship, that is, traits. In contrast, the present chapter has emphasized the need to examine the nature of behavioral criteria from the standpoint of both measurement and theory construction.

References

Block, J. "Advancing the Psychology of Personality: Paradigmatic Shift or Improving the Quality of Research." In D. Magnusson and N. Endler (Eds.), *Personality at the Crossroads: Current Issues in Interactional Psychology.* Hillsdale, N.J.: Erlbaum, 1977.

Bowers, K. S. "Situationism in Psychology: An Analysis and a Critique." *Psychological Review,* 1973, *80,* 307–336.

Dulany, D. E. "Awareness, Rules, and Propositional Control: A Confrontation with S-R Behavior Theory." In D. Horton and T. Dixon (Eds.), *Verbal Behavior and S-R Theory.* Englewood Cliffs, N.J.: Prentice-Hall, 1968.

Edwards, W. "The Theory of Decision Making." *Psychological Bulletin,* 1954, *51,* 380–417.

Endler, N. S. "The Person Versus the Situation—A Pseudo Issue? A Response to Alker." *Journal of Personality,* 1973, *41,* 287–303.

Endler, N. S. "The Role of Person by Situation Interactions in Personality Theory." In F. Weizmann and I. C. Uzgiris (Eds.), *The Structuring of Experience.* New York: Plenum Press, 1976.

Fishbein, M. "An Investigation of the Relationships Between Beliefs About an Object and the Attitude Toward that Object." *Human Relations,* 1963, *16,* 233–240.

Fishbein, M. "Sexual Behavior and Propositional Control." Paper presented at the Psychonomic Society Meetings, 1966.

Fishbein, M. "Attitude and the Prediction of Behavior." In M. Fishbein (Ed.), *Readings in Attitude Theory and Measurement.* New York: Wiley, 1967.

Fishbein, M. "The Prediction of Behaviors from Attitudinal Variables." In C. D. Mortensen and K. K. Sereño (Eds.), *Advances in Communication Research.* New York: Harper & Row, 1973.

Fishbein, M., and Jaccard, J. "Theoretical and Methodological Issues in the Prediction of Family Planning Intentions and Behavior." *Representative Research in Social Psychology,* 1973, *4,* 37–52.

Green, B. F. "Attitude Measurement." In G. Lindzey (Ed.), *Handbook of Social Psychology.* (1st ed.) Reading, Mass.: Addison-Wesley, 1954.

Guttman, L. A. "A Basis for Scaling Qualitative Data." *American Sociological Review,* 1944, *9,* 139–150.

Hornik, J. A. "Two Approaches to Individual Differences in an Expanded Prisoner's Dilemma Game." Unpublished master's thesis, University of Illinois, 1970.

Jaccard, J. J. "Predicting Social Behavior from Personality Traits." *Journal of Research in Personality,* 1974, *7,* 358–367.

Jaccard, J., and Crawford, T. *Psychological Foundations of Attitudes and Behavior.* New York: Free Press, in press.

Jaccard, J., Knox, R., and Brinberg, D. "Prediction of Behavior from Belief: An Extension and Test of a Subjective Probability Model." *Journal of Personality and Social Psychology,* in press.

Lee, W. *Decision Theory and Human Behavior.* New York: Wiley, 1971.

McGrath, J. E. *Social Psychology.* New York: Holt, Rinehart and Winston, 1964.

Magnusson, D., and Endler, N. S. "Interactional Psychology: Present Status and Future Prospects." In D. Magnusson and N. S. Endler (Eds.), *Personality at the Crossroads: Current Issues in Interactional Psychology.* Hillsdale, N.J.: Erlbaum, 1977.

Mischel, W. *Personality and Assessment.* New York: Wiley, 1968.

Mischel, W. "Toward a Cognitive Social Learning Reconceptualization of Personality." *Psychological Review,* 1973, *80,* 252–283.

Mischel, W. *Introduction to Personality.* New York: Holt, Rinehart and Winston, 1976.

Peterson, D. R. *The Clinical Study of Social Behavior.* New York: Appleton-Century-Crofts, 1968.

Rosenberg, M. J. "Cognitive Structure and Attitudinal Effect." *Journal of Abnormal and Social Psychology,* 1956, *53,* 367–372.

Rotter, J. B. "Some Problems and Misconceptions Related to the Construct of Internal Versus External Control of Reinforcement." *Journal of Consulting and Clinical Psychology,* 1975, *43,* 56–67.

Summers, G. F. *Attitude Measurement.* Chicago: Rand McNally, 1970.

Thurstone, L. L., and Chave, E. J. *The Measurement of Attitude.* Chicago: University of Chicago Press, 1929.

Triandis, H. C. *Interpersonal Behavior.* Monterey, Calif.: Brooks/Cole, 1977.

Westoff, C. F., Mishler, E. G., and Kelly, E. L. "Preferences in Size of Family and Eventual Fertility Twenty Years After." *American Journal of Sociology,* 1957, *62,* 491–497.

Wiggins, J. S. *Personality and Prediction: Principles of Personality Assessment.* Reading, Mass.: Addison-Wesley, 1973.

James Jaccard is assistant professor in the Department of Psychological Sciences at Purdue University. He received his Ph.D. from the University of Illinois.

Considerable progress has been made in methodological
approaches to specific person-situation problems,
but solutions to more general issues require greater clarity
about epistemological and metaphysical assumptions.

Epistemology, Metaphysics, and Person-Situation Methodology: Conclusions

Harold L. Raush

Interaction can mean many things, each meaning not very much related to the others (Olweus, 1977; Kulka, p. 55). Methods of study differ in accord with these diverse meanings. A method for studying interaction, defined as meaning the relations among variables which are ascribed to persons, situations, or behaviors will differ from a method designed to study how persons interact with situations to effect environmental change and how situations interact with persons to effect personal change; and both such methods will differ from a method designed to investigate interaction defined as reciprocal, continuous interchange whether between persons—each of whom presents situations for each other—or between persons and environmental situations. And finally there are technological, statistical definitions of interaction, as in analysis of variance, which may or may not relate to the other substantive meanings.

Moreover, specific interests, goals and purposes guide methods. A methodology directed toward studying political attitudes and behavior (Kahle and Berman, p. 23) is apt to differ from a method focusing on relations between persons and social organizations (Kulka, p. 56) and a method seeking to explore the transactions of an intimate relationship (Peterson, p. 38) will differ from both. Specific subject populations of interest also demand differences, or at least variations, in methodology. For example, studies of the development of person-situation relations among infants would undoubtedly require some methodological considerations beyond those presented in the preceding chapters.

Epistemological Assumptions

Explore or Predict. Beyond specific interests, goals, and purposes are the epistemological assumptions which lie at the heart of methodology. Assumptions about the nature of knowledge may seem a far and abstract cry from the operations of "normal science" (Kuhn, 1962). Nonetheless, they profoundly influence what we perceive as scientific problems and the ways we go about solving what we perceive as problems. Is knowledge primarily derived from prediction (deduction, a "context of justification") or is it primarily derived from exploration (induction, a "context of discovery")? Now my guess is none of the authors represented in this sourcebook would opt unequivocally for either one-sided position; as to prediction versus exploration, all might justly claim an "interaction" stance—that scientific development derives from the interplay of both processes. Yet there are—inevitable, I would argue—epistemological biases behind each of the proposed methods. Kahle and Berman's cross-lagged panel correlations and Jaccard's concerns (p. 75) with behavioral criterion measures and moderator variables are directed toward prediction; Peterson's analysis of sequential interchange is expressly exploratory. Kulka's development of alternative models for examining person-environment fit and Jaccard's analysis of possible tracelines between location on a trait dimension and a behavioral act are midway on a prediction-exploration scale. And Bem (p. 7) demonstrates the applicability of Q-sort template matching to both prediction and exploration. (The philosophical differences discussed here might be subjected to a Q-sort template matching analysis with interesting results.)

Jaccard's and Kulka's presentations of alternative models for person-situation fit clearly parallel and supplement one another, though the former derives from scaling theory and the latter from theoretical notions of congruence. One should note that the theoretical possibilities discussed by Kulka and Jaccard pose potential problems for the correlational methods of cross-lagged panel (Kahle and Berman) and template-matching techniques (Bem), if assumptions of linearity and monotonicity are not tenable.

Stability or Change. A second epistemological issue: Is knowledge gained primarily through the study of stable phenomena and constancies or through study of process and change? Are we to focus on continuities or discontinuities? Traditionally, personologists have emphasized constancy and continuity whereas situationists have emphasized change and discontinuity. But this alignment is less a matter of logical necessity than a reflection of our confusions about unit-size and about what constitutes appropriate units for study (see Kulka's discussion, particularly). Certainly, personal life-span data demonstrate coherence and continuity (Block, 1971; Epstein, 1977) as against the specificity of experimentally chosen short-term situations (Mischel, 1977). But if, for example, one chose the life span of cultures as defining the situational unit, there is little doubt that the situation so defined would show coherence and continuity as against the specificity of a personal life span. It is for such reasons—the arbitrariness and incommensurateness of units for defining personological and situational variables—among others (Alker, 1977; Golding, 1975; Olweus, 1977), that analysis of variance designs, while serving well to point to the problems of person-situation relations, have failed to provide answers. It is interesting that none of the methodological approaches that are suggested in this sourcebook as ways of enhancing understanding of person-situation relations are based on the analysis of variance designs which were so characteristic of earlier approaches. Yet, there remain epistemologically-based choices for the investigator—whether to place his or her bets on continuity or change as primary source for understanding. Here again, our authors are not one-sided. All are interested in both the conditions that maintain stability and those that transform relations. Bem uses the template-matching approach to demonstrate consistencies and continuities in both persons and situations. For Peterson as a clinician, possibilities of transformation are most salient. Both Jaccard and Kulka seem to search for continuities, but they suggest methods for examining discontinuities. The cross-lagged panel correlational method of Kahle and Berman serves best only when an assumption of continuity can be met; it can yield causal inference only if the *stationarity* criterion is tenable. It thus becomes inappropriate when theory postulates structural equation change in the relations among phenomena—as in a cognitive stage conception (such as Piaget's), an epigenetic developmental approach (such as Erikson's), or as in most theories of psychotherapy.

Despite these differences of emphasis, on constancy or on change, it is noteworthy that the presentations in the sourcebook individually and conjointly indicate a massive shift away from simplistic questions as to relative importance of personal or situational variables and of the interaction between them. Each author is concerned with the "how" of person-situation relations, with understanding "what goes on." In this sense, "process" has become centrally salient. And as part of that salience, subjective "meaning" has achieved new respectability even in traditional psychology (see also, Bandura, 1978; Mischel, 1977; Neisser, 1976).

Constraint or Freedom. Other issues for methodological consideration lie at the border between epistemological and empirical questions. Is knowledge best gained through maximizing or through minimizing constraints imposed on data? Can we learn more by arranging and limiting antecedent conditions and by restricting units of response than by observing and studying phenomena as they occur in the "natural" world (Willems, 1968)? Such questions are not to be confused with issues of ecological validity. For it is not *logically* necessary that delimitation of antecedent conditions and response units informs us less about phenomena in the "real" world than does study of the phenomena as they present themselves in nature. Partly, it is a matter for proof, and the proof is in the pudding. But partly it is a matter of our differing assumptions about knowledge of human affairs: our assumptions as to the ratio between how much we already know and how much we have yet to learn; our assumptions about the simplicity or complexity of human relations; our assumptions about what is and what is not important. Each of the authors of the preceding chapters is unequivocally committed to a concern with ecological validity. None aim at a "pure" science of person-situation relations that is unconcerned with such relations as they occur in the "real" world. The complexity of the methodologies they examine and propose reflect this concern. The authors do, however, differ in their stances toward the value of constraints on data as part of method for attaining knowledge. Peterson imposes minimal conditions on his subjects and on their responses. The units he develops for analysis derive from the subjects' interactions with one another, rather than from a priori considerations. They have direct and obvious face validity, so much so that one might easily fail to see the simple elegance of the abstractive formulations. Peterson's work, clearly still very much in progress, illustrates both the difficulties and the potential power of a phenomenological approach which leaves subjects relatively free to determine the conditions and nature of their responses. Cross-lagged panel correlation can be, as Kahle and Berman note, relatively free in artificial constraints of antecedent conditions placed on subjects, but once antecedent conditions are defined, the method places sharp constraints on subsequent units of response. In contrast, the analyses presented by both Jaccard and Kulka seem to imply high constraint on antecedent conditions but low restrictions on units of response. The Q-sort employed by Bem does not constrain antecedent conditions, but does constrain responses somewhat; and the experimental "test" situations of Prisoner's Dilemma and forced compliance clearly place high constraint on both antecedent conditions and response units. The power of the Q-sort and template matching lies, I would suggest, in the fact that the set of 100 items was painstakingly developed to provide a comprehensive coverage of personality ascriptions (Block, 1961). It is interesting, then, that the realm of lesser constraint, the Q-sort data, is used to explore and explicate the realm of higher constraint, the experimental data. Note that this ordering represents a radical reversal of usual thinking: that one may develop hypotheses and theories in the less constrained "natural" world, but one then refines hypothesis and theory by means of the more constrained controlled experiment. In Bem's studies it is "real life" data that yield the refinements which are then applied to the cruder, less differentiated experiment. In this sense, Bem's work illustrates not, as he suggests, the ecological validity of the experimental setting, but rather the power of nonexperimental, systematically gathered data to predict and illuminate the more constrained reality of the laboratory. Bem demonstrates that investigation of the general phenomenological world of the subject and that of his or her peers (Bem and Allen, 1974; Bem and Funder, 1978; Bem and Lord, 1979) can tell us what we may expect of him or her in the laboratory and, more importantly, why. Moreover, the studies suggest that such phenomenological investigation can serve as a base for testing the adequacy of divergent theories. Bem, I think, fails to recognize sufficiently this major methodological contribution.

Causal or Systems Analysis. Another influence on methodology deriving from epistemological as well as empirical considerations has to do with fundamental assumptions about causality. Such assumptions are more often implied than explicit. One assumption, traditional to psychology, is of causality as unidirectional. Simply put, there is an A that causes B. As noted particularly by Jaccard and Kulka the directionality need not be linear nor monotonic; and all except the most novice researchers are aware — and often indicate in demurrers — that correlations (and indeed other statistical indexes, except for those which, like cross-lagged panel correlation, are directed specifically at discriminating causal from non-causal relations) do not *prove* causality. Yet the basic notion is that there is a cause (or multiple causes) for any event. For traditional scientists, including psychologists, this is a basic tenet, and the task of science — and of method — is to explicate the cause(s) of a chosen realm of events. Our usual conceptions of experimental design and control are premised on this basic tenet.

A newer, less traditional direction of thought is that of systems theory. Systems theory goes further than rejecting assumptions of unidirectional causality in relation to many phenomena. It suggests that a search for *causal* relations may in itself be fundamentally in error. That is, with respect to many phenomena of interest, we may in such search be tackling the wrong problems or problems so wrongly defined that solution is impossible. By extension, under such circumstances, methods directed toward finding or demonstrating causal relations become not so much wrong as irrelevant. What remains if we discard notions of unidirectional causality? The fear that we thereby forego scientific endeavor is unwarranted. The tasks become that of defining integral systems, of explicating specific and general laws of regulation and organization, and of examining conditions and implications of negative and positive feedback relations and of processes of self-regulation and self-organization (Ashby, 1958, 1968). Among the preceding presentations, Peterson's work comes closest to exemplifying these directions of investigation. His analysis of husband-wife interchanges refers not to causality but to interaction cycles. One may indeed say that a message by a husband—the affect, construal, and expectation that is conveyed—has consequences for the wife's subsequent message, that in this sense A "causes" B. But then, in turn, the wife's message is responded to by the husband. And so on. Peterson (as I read him) is, however, less interested in the chain of specific "causes" and "effects" than in the redundancies and transformations that emerge in the cyclical patterns. Jaccard touches on a systems position in his comments on the "steps" required between the intention of a person to donate blood and the actual act and in his suggestions of a probabilistic sequential analysis. Although he seems to give "causal" primacy to the intention and speaks of such things as learning where to go, arranging transportation, passing a physical, as "intervening factors," the "cause" of the act might be equally and arbitrarily assigned to preceding factors such as the need for blood banks, their existence, personal or public instigations to donate blood, and indeed these, like the intervening factors (as Jaccard notes), may make all the difference between performance and non-performance of the act. A causal analysis would lead to perhaps a modest correlation—varying we should note in different communities and different times—between intention and act. A systems approach would define an "initiating" event (rather than cause) and proceed to investigation of channels, barriers, routes and by-paths to specific outcomes. The causal approach would suggest improving correlations by controlling "intervening factors." The systems analysis would explore how these "factors" work. Kulka also touches on a systems analysis by implication. That is, his differentiation of subjective and objective person and environment, his interest in goodness-of-fit between person and environment, and his emphasis on alternative modes for analyzing person-environment congruence suggest a systems rather than causal approach.

Metaphysical Assumptions

Kulka's comments on the distinction between *objective* and *subjective* person and between *objective* and *subjective* environment bring me to the problem that will occupy the remainder of this chapter. I have suggested the intimate linkage between methodology and the realm of substantive interest and between methodology and epistemological positions. Here I would turn to a problem that is fundamentally metaphysical in nature. Specifically, it has to do with how we conceive of persons and situations, that is, our theories, explicit or implicit, as to the nature of human relations with the world.

Fiske (1977) notes the current sophistication of methodology in studying the interactions between persons and their environments, and, indeed, the chapters of this sourcebook extend this sophistication considerably. But Fiske (p. 285) comments further on the lack of basic scientific foundation, and he notes that, lacking basic theory, our studies become limited to a search for empirical pragmatic relationships. Such lacks and limitations reflect, I might suggest, our basic confusions as to what constitutes persons and what constitutes situations. For though we can agree on the Lewinian equation that $B = f(P, E)$ — that behavior is a function of the person and the environment — at other than the most general level, each of the terms presents us with massive difficulties. For purposes of the following discussion I shall omit specific considerations of behavior (B). For that side of the equation, Jaccard's comments on a taxonomy of behavioral measures are particularly relevant; moreover, implications for conceptualization of behavior should be readily apparent in what follows. In any case, I shall concentrate on the P, E or P, S (situation) part.

The Person. In psychological discourse it is entirely unclear what we mean by and what we set as the boundaries of person. Kulka, as noted, distinguishes between "the *objective person,* referring to the objectively demonstrable characteristics of the person (needs, values, abilities, and other attitudes which are relatively enduring), independent of his or her perceptions and the *subjective person,* the individual's perceptions or cognitions of his or her objective characteristics (the self-concept or self-identity of the person)" (p. 56). Bem, in employing self Q-sort and sorts by peers, implies a similar distinction, and Jaccard touches on this discrimination in referring to *personal* versus *normative* considerations. "Person" may thus refer to either objective or subjective assessments, or to both, or indeed, as Bem's work suggests, to the conjunction or disjunction between the two.

Furthermore, the quote taken from Kulka speaks of relatively enduring attitudes in relation to defining the *objective person,* and implies relative endurance (self-concept or self-identity) in defining the *subjective person.* Personologists, in their search for stabilities and consistencies, would generally agree with a criterion of relative endurance for defining "person." Yet, that leaves momentary states, moods, needs, motives and interests — which clearly influence behavior — in limbo, belonging neither to person nor situation.

Finally, the very meanings of *objective* and *subjective* are metaphysically obscure (Gibbs, 1979). Is an idea, a thought, a feeling, a dream last night, or a goal, *in me,* or is it *out there?* Does it shift from being subjective to becoming objective when it is stated to others, or when others can argue that it is there, or when it is measurable? And which others and what sort of objective demonstrability are we speaking of? Would not judgments of my motives and characteristics surely differ when made from a Marxist, a social learning, or a psychoanalytic frame of reference? Or is objective to be put in the same language—by those who more or less use terms as I do—as subjective? Such questions may be seen as philosophical, but they determine empirical studies, differences in methods, analyses, results, and interpretations.

The Situation. What we mean by situation and what we set as situational boundaries is similarly entirely unclear. Kulka distinguishes between "the *objective environment,* which includes aspects of the physical and social world that exist independently of the person's perception of them, and the subjective environment, representing the person's perceptions and cognitions of relevant aspects of his or her objective environment" (p. 56). Magnusson (1978) also differentiates between the *objective* and the *psychological* situation, and he reviews an extensive literature relating to this distinction. As in the case of objective and subjective person, the distinction carries an immediate intuitive sense, yet becomes ambiguous when applied to specific instances. For one thing, situation may and has been used to refer to events ranging from specific stimuli to total environments and "life situations." For another, some phenomena seem unlocatable in this ostensibly universally encompassing scheme. For example, is my past life history a situation? Does it become objective when described by others? And, again, which others? Is an intimate relationship, as Peterson suggests, a situation? Is the grammatical object of any sentence a situation? When I say, "I must think about my future," is "my future" a situation, and is it to be categorized as objective or subjective? Similar questions arise when couples say "we work on our relationship," or when a group says, "we must defend the rights of free speech." And finally, if the *subjective environment* is the person's perceptions and cognitions, the conceptual border separating *person* from *situation* fades to obscurity.

The Interaction. Irrespective of the objectivity or subjectivity of persons and situations, there is continuous ongoing commerce between the two. Persons do not exist apart from situational contexts; such contexts are not only represented in the immediate and visible, but also in the historic times and cultures within which lives are lived. Similarly, for psychology at least, situations do not exist apart from persons engaged with them. Persons select, engender, and create situations (Bowers, 1973; Wachtel, 1973, 1977; see also Magnusson and

Endler, 1977, p. 20). Situations similarly select, engender, and create persons (Barker, 1968; Moos and Insel, 1974; Proshansky, Ittelson and Rivlis, 1970; and Tolstoy's *War and Peace,* particularly the final chapter); certainly, one's dispositions and traits have been created, at least in part and in any theory, by the past situations one has encountered. Moreover, the process is a continuous, conjoint, and often transformative one. We enter into and create situations to *effect* change: "Few would engage in an argument, a political struggle, a new job, a field of research, a relationship without hoping to induce personal or situational transformations" (Raush, 1977a, p. 295). So, too, situations choose persons to *effect* change: a new ballplayer for a losing team, or a new executive for a changing institution. The change may be the reinstatement of a threatened homeostatic balance or it may represent a morphogenesis (Buckley, 1967; Speer, 1970) to a new set of conditions. A conception of this process requires, as Bowers (1977) notes (quoting Overton, 1973), a shift from the *additive* paradigm which views interaction as the summative effect of antecedent variables to an *interactive* paradigm in which "because the organism affects the environment affecting the organism in ongoing sequences of exchange, [there is] little truck for hard and fast distinctions between antecedent conditions and behavioral outcomes" (Bowers, 1977, p. 76).

Conceptual and Methodological Requirements for a "Truly" Interactive Paradigm

A truly interactive paradigm requires that person and situation not be " . . . considered as two autonomously preexisting units interacting with each other at a given moment, but that both . . . only function and exist as two interdependent poles of a unitary behavioral process" (Nuttin, 1977, p. 201). Although person and situation *can* be conceptualized as relatively independent, when the contextual frame is that of the psychological functioning of the *total* organism they can no longer be thought of as independent. As with, for example, circulating and respiratory systems when viewed from the context of an organism as a whole, person and situation became *quasi-independent* subsystems within a larger system (Raush, 1977a). That larger system is not person *and* situation, not even person-*in*-situation, but rather the *person-situation system* (including emergent behavior) itself.

The Person-Situation System. This is not to deny an "objective" reality to either persons or situations. Metaphysically, I may assume a "real" world of bounded others and bounded situations, and I may assume that our physical and psychological boundaries as persons are "real." Such metaphysical notions derive, I would suggest, not from my "knowing" these realities as given, but rather from my activity in the world from which this "knowing" emerges. My conception of myself as person is an abstractive product from the flux of past and ongoing person-situation relations: My individual self is that which through memory, conscious and unconscious, has continuity through person-situation relations. My conception of situation is similarly an abstractive product: that which is not constrained simply by my memory or wishes, but rather represents the person-situation relations that I must act upon to maintain or transform. Even when I speak of changing my "self" in some way, that "self" becomes "objectified" as part of a person-situation system.

The point of these philosophical speculations is to note that not only do we construct persons ("selves") and situations which then become real to us (Berger and Luckmann, 1967), but also that the "objective" is created and recreated by the "subjective" and vice versa in a continuing interplay (Raush, 1977b, pp. 184–186). We "know" neither the "objective" person nor the "objective" situation. We "know" only the interaction. Gibbs (1979, p. 133) in discussing objectivism and subjectivism quotes Dewey on "the recurrent modes of interaction taking place between what we term organism, on the one side, and environment, on the other. This interaction is the primary fact . . . only by analysis and selective abstraction can we differentiate the actual occurrence into two factors, one called organism and the other, the environment" (Dewey, 1930, p. 411). Indeed, this point of view was reflected in Dewey's (1896) classic paper on the reflex arc, and it has been reiterated periodically by modern investigators (Bowers, 1973; Carson, 1969; Gibbs, 1979).

Acceptance of the person-situation system as our primary data has implications for methodology. For one thing, the distinction between persons and situations and between objective and subjective would lose their salience. Our questions would shift toward a more direct examination of the person-situation system. For example, we would ask about the extensivity of channels between subsystems and among parts of subsystems, or the extent to which variables are so "richly joined" that the slightest change will have a massive effect or so "poorly joined" that a change has only local and highly specific effect (Ashby, 1968; Magnusson, 1978). We would be concerned with the disjunctions as compared to the isomorphisms between subsystems and among parts of subsystems, that is, the tensions or lack of tensions within a person-situation system. We would be interested in the permeability and flexibility of boundaries between subsystems and among parts of subsystems. We would look for positive and negative feedback processes. And we would attempt to discover the generative rules and required redundancies of particular person-situation systems (Argyle, 1977). In a sense, these directions—some of which I have discussed elsewhere (Raush, 1977a)—elaborate Kulka's concerns with "fit" between person and environment, but by foregoing sharp distinctions between person and situation and between objective and subjective they direct our attentions to the more salient problems of conditions for both stability and change.

"Personal" and "Consensual" Orientations. As to "persons" and "situations," I prefer to think of these as *orientations* that we take, whether as participants in our existence in the world or as investigators. We hold "personal"—rather than subjective—views of ourselves and of situations. There are also what might be termed "consensual"—rather than objective—views that others hold of us and of situations, as illustrated in Bem's studies; and as noted above, such a consensus is always by particular persons, located in a particular time and culture. The isomorphisms or disjunctions between "personal" and "consensual" views of persons or situations become, as suggested above, conditions for investigating stability and change. What counts is not the subjectivity or objectivity, but the fit, the tensions, the capacities and limitations of the system to maintain itself or to change, and the dialectics of this process.

Language. As to the need for a language for person-situation systems, it seems to me that (beyond the need for adequate terms for structure and process concepts—a severe enough problem) ordinary language, when used with care and thought, can serve for describing content. Bem's work shows that situations can be described in "person" terms, and he suggests studies whereby persons could be described in "situation" terms, but neither of these would achieve the level of terms in common that he would most favor. Moreover, the search for a special taxonomy of situations (Frederiksen, 1972) offers us no greater possibilities of success than our currently inadequate taxonomies of persons. As Mischel (1977) notes: "It is important to avoid emerging simply with a trait psychology of situations, in which events and settings, rather than people, are merely given different labels. The task of naming situations cannot substitute for the job of analyzing *how* conditions and environments interact with the people in them" (p. 338).

Temporal Process. A final methodological requirement of the interactive paradigm suggested above is the need for greater recognition of and emphasis on a temporal frame of reference for person-situation systems. Such systems evolve, reiterate, and perhaps transform over time through sequences of successive steps and through recurrent cycles of interchange (Gibbs, 1979; Gottman, 1973; Jaccard, p. 75; Peterson, p. 35; Raush, 1972). Clearly, we need more definitive methods for analyzing these aspects. But failure to recognize the temporal frame induces research to a static model of fixed labels, unproductive for understanding, of minimal use in effecting personal or social change, and untrue to our lives in a world in which our interactions—with ourselves, with others, and with events—are framed in time.

Conclusion

The advances in methodology represented in the preceding chapters range from presentations of specific techniques for investigating person-situation interactions to presentations of the generic problems and issues in this vital area of research. The specific methods are indeed new directions, going beyond the analysis of variance designs which have characterized the field and entering more deeply into the core of questions about how persons and situations interact. The theoretical discussions face issues that have been by-passed or ignored previously, and they too suggest new directions for research. Although the diversity of the substantive problems tackled and the methodologies offered in these chapters permit no simple coalescent summarization, that diversity insures that the investigator, interested in a particular research issue, will find in these contents substance that speaks to this issue. Thus, although we have not yet come near to solving the general problems of person-situation relations, we have come a ways toward examining and investigating specific research questions. Solutions—if there are any—to the more general methodological questions will, I suggest, require more searching examination of the epistemological and metaphysical assumptions which lie at the very heart of our conceptions of person-situation interaction.

References

Alker, H. A. "Beyond ANOVA Psychology in the Study of Person-Situation Interactions." In D. Magnusson and N. S. Endler (Eds.), *Personality at the Crossroads: Current Issues in Interactional Psychology.* Hillsdale, N.J.: Erlbaum, 1977.

Argyle, M. "Predictive and Generative Rules Models of PxS Interaction." In D. Magnusson and N. S. Endler (Eds.), *Personality at the Crossroads: Current Issues in Interactional Psychology.* Hillsdale, N.J.: Erlbaum, 1977.

Ashby, W. R. *An Introduction to Cybernetics.* New York: Wiley, 1958.

Ashby, W. R. "Principles of the Self-Organizing System." In W. Buckley (Ed.), *Modern Systems Research for the Behavioral Scientist.* Chicago: Aldine, 1968.

Bandura, A. "The Self System in Reciprocal Determinism." *American Psychologist,* 1978, *33,* 344–358.

Barker, R. G. *Ecological Psychology.* Stanford, Calif.: Stanford University Press, 1968.

Bem, D. J., and Allen, A. "On Predicting Some of the People Some of the Time: The Search for Cross-Situational Consistencies in Behavior." *Psychological Review,* 1974, *81,* 506–520.

Bem, D. J., and Funder, D. C. "Predicting More of the People More of the Time: Assessing the Personality of Situations." *Psychological Review,* 1978, *85,* 485–501.

Bem, D. J., and Lord, C. G. "The Template-Matching Technique: A Proposal for Probing the Ecological Validity of Experimental Settings in Social Psychology." *Journal of Personality and Social Psychology,* 1979, *37,* 833–846.

Berger, P. L., and Luckmann, T. *The Social Construction of Reality.* New York: Anchor Books, 1967.

Block, J. *The Q-Sort Method in Personality Assessment and Psychiatric Research.* Springfield, Ill.: Charles C. Thomas, 1961.

Block, M. *Lives Through Time.* Berkeley, Calif.: Bancroft Books, 1971.

Bowers, K. S. "Situationism in Psychology: An Analysis and Critique." *Psychological Review,* 1973, *80,* 307–336.

Bowers, K. S. "There's More to Iago than Meets the Eye: A Clinical Account of Personal Consistency." In D. Magnusson and N. S. Endler (Eds.), *Personality at the Crossroads: Current Issues in Interactional Psychology.* Hillsdale, N.J.: Erlbaum, 1977.

Buckley, W. *Sociology and Modern Systems Theory.* Englewood Cliffs, N.J.: Prentice-Hall, 1967.

Carson, R. C. *Interaction Concepts of Personality.* Chicago: Aldine, 1969.

Dewey, J. "The Reflex Arc Concept in Psychology." *Psychological Review,* 1896, *3,* 357–370.

Dewey, J. "Conduct and Experience." In C. Murchison (Ed.), *Psychologies of 1930.* Worcester, Mass.: Clark University Press, 1930.

Epstein, S. "Traits Are Alive and Well." In D. Magnusson and N. S. Endler (Eds.), *Personality at the Crossroads: Current Issues in Interactional Psychology.* Hillsdale, N.J.: Erlbaum, 1977.

Fiske, D. W. "Personologies, Abstractions, and Interactions." In D. Magnusson and N. S. Endler (Eds.), *Personality at the Crossroads: Current Issues in Interactional Psychology.* Hillsdale, N.J.: Erlbaum, 1977.

Frederiksen, N. "Toward a Taxonomy of Situations." *American Psychologist,* 1972, *27,* 114–123.

Gibbs, J. C. "The Meaning of Ecologically Oriented Inquiry in Contemporary Psychology." *American Psychologist,* 1979, *34,* 127–140.

Golding, S. L. "Flies in the Ointment: Methodological Problems in the Analysis of the Percentage of Variance Due to Persons and Situations." *Psychological Bulletin,* 1975, *82,* 278–288.

Gottman, J. M. "N-of-one and N-of-two Research in Psychotherapy." *Psychological Bulletin,* 1973, *80,* 93–105.

Kuhn, T. S. *The Structure of Scientific Revolutions.* Chicago: University of Chicago Press, 1962.

Magnusson, D. "On the Psychological Situation." University of Stockholm, Department of Psychology Report No. 544, 1978.

Magnusson, D., and Endler, N. S. "Interactional Psychology: Present Status and Future Prospects." In D. Magnusson and N. S. Endler (Eds.), *Personality at the Crossroads: Current Issues in Interactional Psychology.* Hillsdale, N.J.: Erlbaum, 1977.

Mischel, W. "The Interaction of Person and Situation." In D. Magnusson and N. S. Endler (Eds.), *Personality at the Crossroads: Current Issues in Interactional Psychology.* Hillsdale, N.J.: Erlbaum, 1977.

Moos, R. H., and Insel, P. M. *Issues in Social Ecology.* Palo Alto, Calif.: National Press Books, 1974.

Neisser, U. *Cognition and Reality: Principles and Implications of Cognitive Psychology.* San Francisco: W. H. Freeman, 1976.

Nuttin, J. R. "A Conceptual Frame of Personality-World Interaction: A Relational Theory." In D. Magnusson and N. S. Endler (Eds.), *Personality at the Crossroads: Current Issues in Interactional Psychology.* Hillsdale, N.J.: Erlbaum, 1977.

Olweus, D. "A Critical Analysis of the 'Modern' Interactionist Position." In D. Magnusson and N. S. Endler (Eds.), *Personality at the Crossroads: Current Issues in Interactional Psychology.* Hillsdale, N.J.: Erlbaum, 1977.

Overton, W. F. "On the Assumptive Base of the Nature-Nurture Controversy: Additive Versus Interactive Conceptions." *Human Development,* 1973, *16,* 74–89.

Proshansky, H. M., Ittelson, W. H., and Rivlis, L. S. (Eds.). *Environmental Psychology: Man and His Physical Setting.* New York: Holt, Rinehart and Winston, 1970.

Raush, H. L. "Process and Change: A Markov Model for Interaction." *Family Process,* 1972, *11,* 275-298.

Raush, H. L. "Paradox, Levels, and Junctures in Person-Situation Systems." In D. Magnusson and N. S. Endler (Eds.), *Personality at the Crossroads: Current Issues in Interactional Psychology.* Hillsdale, N.J.: Erlbaum, 1977a.

Raush, H. L. "Orientations to the Close Relationship." In G. Levinger and H. L. Raush (Eds.), *Close Relationships: Perspectives on the Meaning of Intimacy.* Amherst: University of Massachusetts Press, 1977b.

Speer, D. C. "Family Systems: Morphostasis and Morphogenesis or 'Is Homeostasis Enough?' " *Family Process,* 1970, *9,* 259-278.

Wachtel, P. L. "Psychodynamics, Behavior Therapy, and the Implacable Experimenter: An Inquiry into the Consistency of Personality." *Journal of Abnormal Psychology,* 1973, *82,* 324-334.

Wachtel, P. L. "Interaction Cycles, Unconscious Processes, and the Person-Situation Issue." In D. Magnusson and N. S. Endler (Eds.), *Personality at the Crossroads: Current Issues in Interactional Psychology.* Hillsdale, N.J.: Erlbaum, 1977.

Willems, E. P. "Planning a Rationale for Naturalistic Research." In E. P. Willems and H. L. Raush (Eds.), *Naturalistic Viewpoints in Psychological Research.* New York: Holt, Rinehart and Winston, 1968.

Harold L. Raush teaches psychology at the University of Massachusetts in Amherst. With E. P. Willems, he edited Naturalistic Viewpoints in Psychological Research.

Index

A

Affect, 43–46
Aggregation, defined, 20
Alexander, C. N., 6, 13
Alker, H. A., 95, 104
Allen, A., 13, 68, 69, 97, 104
Andrews, F. M., 18, 31, 61, 68, 71
Argyle, M., 102, 104
Ashby, W. R., 98, 102, 104
Autocorrelation, 19, 24, 30

B

Bandura, A., 95, 104
Barker, R. G., 101, 104
Bartlett, C. J., 59, 71
Bateson, G., 44, 46, 53
Baumrind, D., 4, 13
Beavin, J. H., 43, 54
Behavioral decisions: analysis of, 79–82; determinants of, 83–85; and intervening factors, 80–81; measurement issues and, 79–80; and personality, 81–82
Behavioral measures: analysis of, 73–81; taxonomy of, 74–89
Bem, D. J., vii, 1–15, 60, 68, 69, 94, 95, 96, 97, 99, 103, 104
Bereiter, C., 61, 69
Berger, P. L., 102, 105
Berman, J. J., vii, 17–32, 94, 95, 96
Bernal, M. E., 51, 53
Berne, E., 43, 53
Blau, P. M., 61, 62, 69
Block, J., 2, 3, 8, 10, 11n, 14, 73, 74, 77, 90, 96, 105
Block, J. H., 8, 14
Block, M., 95, 105
Bohrnstedt, G. W., 61, 69
Bonoma, T. V., 6, 15
Bowers, K. S., 28, 31, 73, 90, 100, 101, 102, 105
Brewer, M., 28, 31
Brinberg, D., 79, 91
Buckley, W., 101, 105

C

Calsyn, R. J., 27, 31
Campbell, D. T., 18, 20, 28, 29, 31, 38, 53

Caplan, R. D., 56, 58, 69
Carlsmith, J. M., 5, 6, 14
Carson, R., 37, 53, 102, 105
Carver, R. P., 30, 31
Cause, defined, 19–20
Chave, E. J., 86, 88, 91
Chayes, F., 61, 69
Christensen, A., 50–51, 53
Cobb, S., 55–56, 59, 60, 61, 69
Cognitive dissonance theory, 5, 6
Cohen, J., 47, 53
Construal, 44–46
Cook, T. D., 20, 31
Correlation, defined, 19
Crano, W. D., 18, 28, 31
Crawford, T., 91
Cronbach, L. J., 61, 62, 68, 69
Cross-lagged, defined, 18
Cross-lagged panel correlation (CLPC): analysis of, 17–32; assumptions in, 20–22; defined, 18; limitations and advantages of, 28–30; method of, 18–22; and time lags, 27, 29; uses of, 26–28

D

Delay of gratification, 8–11
DeSoto, C. B., viii, ix
Dewey, J., 102, 105
Douglas, R. L., 4, 14
Dulany, D. E., 79, 90
Duncan, O. D., 61, 62, 69
Duncan, Jr., S., viii, ix

E

Ecological validity, 4–5, 96
Edwards, W., 78, 90
Ekehammer, B., 59, 69
Endler, N. S., viii, ix, 1, 14, 35, 53, 90, 100, 105
Epstein, S., 95, 105
Expectation, 44–46

F

Feather, N. T., 55, 56, 59, 61, 68, 69
Feld, S., 56, 59, 60, 71
Feldman, K. A., 62, 63, 67, 69

Festinger, L., 5, 14
Fishbein, M., 74, 78, 79, 80, 83, 84, 90
Fiske, D. W., viii, ix, 38, 53, 99, 105
Forced compliance experiment, 5-7
Frederiksen, N., 1, 14, 103, 105
French, Jr., R. P., 55-56, 59, 60, 61, 69
Fuguitt, G. V., 61, 69
Funder, D. C., 1, 4, 5, 6-7, 8, 9n, 10, 13, 97, 104
Furby, L., 61, 62, 69

G

Getzels, J. W., 56, 70
Gibbs, J. C., 100, 102, 103, 105
Gleser, G., 61, 68, 69
Golding, S. L., 95, 105
Gottman, J. M., 103, 105
Graham, W. K., 60, 70
Green, B. F., 86, 90
Guttman, L. A., 89, 90

H

Hackman, J. R., 60, 70
Hall, D. T., 60, 63, 67, 68, 70
Harackiewicz, J. M., 18, 20, 31
Hargis, D., 7
Harris, R. J., 61, 70
Harris, T. A., 43, 53
Harrison, R. V., 56, 58, 59, 60, 70
Helson, H., 67, 70
Hoffman, C., 12
Hogan, R., viii, ix
Holland, C. H., 4, 14
Holland, J. L., 56, 70
Homans, G. C., 37, 53
Hops, H., 41, 50, 54
Hornik, J. A., 80, 90
Hulin, C. L., 68, 70
Hunt, J. M., 35, 53

I

Imparato, N., 61, 70
Insel, P. M., 101, 105
Interaction: aspects of, 37; cycles of, 48-49; defined, 55; metaphysical assumptions on, 100-101; process of, 47-49; recrods of, 38-47; requirements of paradigm for, 101-104; sequence of, 36-37
Interpersonal relationships, study of: analysis of, 33-54; future of, 49-53; method for, 34-38
Ittelson, W. H., 101, 105

J

Jaccard, J. J., viii, 73-91, 94, 95, 96, 97, 98, 99, 103
Jackson, D. D., 43, 46, 53, 54
Jenkins, G. D., 59, 70
Jorgenson, G. W., 58, 70

K

Kagan, N., 51, 53
Kahana, E., 56, 63, 67, 70
Kahle, L. R., vii-ix, 17-32, 55n, 94, 95, 96
Kahn, R. L., 60, 61, 69
Kelley, H. H., 4, 14, 37, 54
Kelly, E. L., 79, 91
Kennedy, T., 46, 54
Kenny, D. A., 17n, 18, 19-20, 21, 24, 25, 27, 28, 29, 30, 31
Kessler, R. C., 61, 70
Klingel, D. M., 56, 58, 70
Knight, G. W., 6, 13
Knox, R., 79, 91
Knox, R. E., 4, 14
Kuhn, T. S., 94, 105
Kulka, R. A., viii, 55-71, 93, 94, 95, 96, 97, 98, 99, 100, 103

L

Lawler, E. E., III, 56, 60, 61, 70
Lee, W., 78, 91
Lepper, M. R., 6
Lewin, K., 60, 70, 99
Lieberson, S., 61, 69
Locke, E. A., 56, 59, 70
Lord, C. G., 4, 5, 7-8, 13, 14, 97, 104
Lord, F. M., 61, 70
Luckmann, T., 102, 105

M

McClintock, C. G., 4, 14
McGrath, J. E., 76, 91
McGuire, W. J., viii, ix, 4, 14, 29, 31
Magnusson, D., viii, ix, 1, 14, 73, 91, 100, 102, 105
Mann, D. W., 56, 58, 70
Markman, H., 47, 53
Marks, E., 60, 70
Martin, B., 8, 14
Martin, S., 51, 53
Maxfield, D., 7
Messick, D. M., 4, 14

Mikes, P. S., 68, 70
Mischel, W., viii, ix, 8, 9, 14, 22, 26, 31, 35, 51, 53, 73, 74, 91, 95, 103, 105
Mishler, E. G., 79, 91
Mixed-motive game, 4–5, 7–8
Moos, R. H., 1, 14, 56, 59, 60, 71, 101, 105

N

Neisser, U., 95, 105
Nemeth, C., 4, 14
Newcomb, T. M., 62, 63, 69
Notarious, C., 47, 53
Nunnally, J. C., 61, 67, 68, 71
Nuttin, J. R., 101, 105

O

Olson, D. H., 51, 53
Olweus, D., 55, 71, 93, 95, 105
Orne, M. T., 4, 14
Overton, W. F., 101, 105

P

Padawer-Singer, A., viii, ix
Page, M. M., 29, 31
Panel, defined, 18–19
Patterson, G. R., 41, 50, 54
Pelz, D. C., 18, 31, 61, 68, 71
Person, metaphysical assumptions about, 99–100
Person-environment (P-E) fit: analysis of, 55–71; and commensurate units, 60–61; issues in, 58–68; measures of, 61–62; model of, 56–58; quantitative representations of, 62–67; and strain, 57–58; subjective or objective measures of, 59–60
Person-situation interactions: and behavioral measures, 73–91; conclusions about, 93–106; congruence in, 55–71; and cross-lagged panel correlation, 17–32; epistemology and, 94–98; metaphysical assumptions about, 98–101; in natural settings, 33–54; re-emergence of interest in, vii; system in, 101–103; template-matching assessment of, 1–15
Pervin, L. A., 1, 14, 56, 59, 60, 68, 71
Peterson, D. R., viii, 33–54, 73, 91, 93, 94, 95, 96, 98, 100, 103

Proshansky, H. M., 101, 105
Pruitt, D. G., 4, 14

Q

Q-sort technique: heuristic value of, 7–11; and template construction, 2–4, 6, 12–13
Quasi-stationarity, 21, 25

R

Rabunsky, C., 51, 53
Ransen, D., 7
Raush, H. L., viii, 38, 41, 47, 54, 93–106
Retrospection, defined, 20
Ring, K., 4, 14
Ringuette, E. L., 46, 54
Riskin, J., 43, 53
Rivlis, L. S., 101, 105
Robinson, D. L., 47, 54
Robinson, W. S., 61, 71
Rodgers, W., 55–56, 59, 60, 61, 69
Rosenberg, M. J., 6, 14, 83, 91
Ross, L., 26, 31
Rotter, J. B., 84, 91
Rozelle, R. M., 18, 29, 31

S

Satir, V., 43, 53
Schlenker, B. R., 6, 15
Schneider, B., 59, 71
Schuessler, K., 61, 71
Schuham, A. I., 46, 54
Self-perception theory, 5–6
Self-presentation theory, 6
Sells, S. B., 35, 54
Single act criteria, prediction of, 78–79, 85–89
Situation: metaphysical assumptions about, 100; and template matching, 5–7, 12–13
Solano, C., viii, ix
Southwood, K. E., 55, 71
Speer, D. C., 101, 106
Stanley, J. C., 18, 31
Stationarity, 21, 24
Staub, E., 7, 15
Stern, G., 56, 62, 71
Stimulus condition self-selection, 22–26
Strodtbeck, F. T., 37–38, 54
Summers, G. F., 88, 91
Suppes, P., 20, 31
Synchronous correlation, 19, 24, 29

T

Tedeschi, J. T., 6, 15
Template-matching technique: analysis
   of, 1–15; concept of, 2; constructing
   templates for, 2–4
Terrill, J., 41, 54
Terrill, R., 41, 54
Thibaut, J. W., 37, 54
Thurstone, L. L., 86, 88, 89, 91
Traceline, 86–89
Trait: concept of, 73–74, 76; and single-
   act criteria prediction, 85–89
Triandis, H. C., 78, 91

V

Variables, in cross-lagged panel correlation, 19, 27–28
Veroff, J., 56, 59, 60, 71

W

Wachtel, P. L., 22, 31, 100, 106
Wainer, H., 67, 68, 71
Watzlawick, P., 43, 54
Weiss, R. L., 41, 50, 54
Westoff, C. F., 79, 91
Willems, E. P., 96, 106
Wylie, R. C., 62, 71